IN LOVE AND WORK
Poems

Fred Yager
Jan Yager

"This beautiful book of poems is a peek into the lives of a loving couple. The poems are a diary of feelings before and after Fred and Jan Yager became husband and wife. Some poems are fun and lighthearted; others are heart wrenching. This is the case in Fred's story of witnessing 9/11 firsthand. Reading these poems will take you through a range of emotions. In the end, you will be glad to have met the Yagers if only through their words."
—Beverly Solomon, creative director for artist Pablo Solomon

Hannacroix Creek Books, Inc.
Stamford, Connecticut

In Love and Work: Poems
Published by Hannacroix Creek Books, Inc.

Copyright © 2026, 2014 Fred Yager and Jan Yager
All rights reserved.

Cover photos of Fred Yager and Jan Yager (the former
J.L. Janet Lee Barkas) Contributed photos
Wedding photo, December 1984
Updated photo, November 2025
(Photo credit: Jeff Yager)

Hannacroix Creek Books, Inc.
1127 High Ridge Road
#110
Stamford, CT 06905 USA
http://www.hannacroixcreekbooks.com
hannacroix@aol.com

ISBN: 978-1-938998-61-4 (trade paperback)

CONTENTS

A Note from Jan	1
Remembering Mom by Jan Yager	2
Part One **by Fred Yager**	14
Today	15
September 11, 2001	16
9/11 Ten Years After: Reflections of a Survivor	17
Twenty One Years	23
Writing	25
Hotels	26
The Ballad of Evil Ely	27
A Secret Birthday Poem	30
A Cold Day in December	31
Another Year Flies By	32
All You Are	33
Beach Fortress	34
One Night in Golden Gate Park	35
A Quiet Day	37
Silent Shower	38
Half Kids	39
Lonesome Roads	41
Two Sides of the Rainbow	42
Another Night of Drinking in a Dusty Texas Town	44
Vietnam	46
San Francisco, Summer of '67	48
I've Just Been Wondering	50
Solitary Confinement	51
Overexposed: A Dream	52
Winter Dreams	53

The Fire Next Time	55
It Scares Me	56
Blue White	57
Fractured	58
Just Ain't Around Anymore	59
We Knew	60
Running Away	61
I Found You	62
So Can I	63
Lonely Eyes	64
Meditation	65
With Child	66
I've Got a Song	67
To Be Understood	68
Bringing Love Close	69
The Listener	70
Happy Valentine's Day	71
Forty-one Years	72
Part Two by Jan Yager	**73**
Writing in a Fish Bowl	74
February 14th	75
Slipping Away	76
On Our Fifth Anniversary	79
The Surprise	80
Your Valentine's Day Gift to Me	83
Happy Father's Day, Daddy, Up in Heaven	86
My New Friend	89
Momisms	90
Sis	96
Chance Meeting	99
Grief	103
A Grandparent's Love	106

Returning to My Work as an Artist	107
The Victim	110
Why I Write	111
For the Love of a Cat	114
Friendshifts	117
911	119
The Single Hours	123
Deadlines	125
Self-love	127
In Quarantine	128
A Disagreement with Homan's Exchange Theory of Satiation	129
Missing You	130
Ode to Love	132
New Romance	133
Love Slipped Away	135
Nature's Lisp	139
Winter	140
The Hardest Kind of Love	141
The Bird Feeder	156
If Only He Wanted to Be With Me	157
The Idea Thief	159
Children's Day	160
Growing Up	162
The Thief	163
Anti-War Song	164
Adolescence	165
Who Am I?	167
Responsibility	168
Unspoken Love	169
The Cone	170
Reversal	171
Raravis	172

Second Chance   173
I am a Jew   174

About the Authors   178

A Note from Jan

This book has been more than twelve years in the making for many reasons. The first one is that I decided to postpone publishing a collection of our poetry until at least a couple of the poems in Fred's part of the anthology were about me and not just from before we met about other women from his past. It took a while for that to happen but as you've seen, Fred has written several poems about me related to Valentine's Day, our wedding anniversary, and my birthday.

With that goal accomplished, what were my new excuses for delaying publication of this collection? Besides the defense of putting other more practical projects and professional commitments before publishing this poetry collection, I found myself resisting its publication of these very personal poems because it turned out to be a lot harder to share our poems about love and work with "the world" than I thought it would be.

I'm a great believer in looking at the "trigger" events to why we do something we've been putting off for a long time. There are, of course, conscious triggers and unconscious ones. In the case of this collection of poetry, the conscious trigger to finally publish these poems was the death of my beloved 90-year-old Mother. I wrote a poem about my Mom, "Remembering Mom," that I read at her memorial service and that was a very powerful and positive experience for me. The feedback I received at the time, as well as in the days afterwards, and from those to whom the poem was e-mailed, reinforced for me the power of poetry to express our deepest thoughts and feelings, and also to act as a catharsis, not just for the author, but for the listener. I already knew the benefits of sharing poetry in dealing with illness, death, and grief; Fred and I had contributed to a collection of poems on those topics, *The Healing Power of Creative Mourning: Poems,* that was published in 2000, four years after my father had died.

I am including that poem about my mother, "Remembering Mom," in this collection, *In Love and Work*, since I prefer not to return to the previous collection *The Healing Power of Creative Mourning*; that collection still stands on its own. For this book, I added photographs throughout my poem "Remembering Mom." I predict my Mom, who was truly a beautiful woman "inside and outside," as the saying goes, would have been pleased that I'm sharing her physical beauty with the world, through photographs of her as well as through my words.

Here is my poem, "Remembering Mom."

REMEMBERING MOM

My Mom's illness made me very sad for her.
This once vital woman who had become progressively so dependent.

But she loved it when I played music
And I moved her arms up and down
To the rhythm of the music
As she sat in her wheelchair.
And she smiled because of the music
Because the movement and the music made her happy
This talented woman for whom music was always so important
This woman who wrote original songs
And sang and played the piano by ear.

I loved my mother
And I feel blessed that we had so much time together these last seven years
Especially since she moved to my hometown
Six years ago
Even though the years were hard on her physically and mentally.

She complained initially but ironically
As her incurable disease of Lewy Body Dementia progressed,
She became completely accepting of her situation.
I always told her that she was a role model to me and to so many others
Of how to handle adversity
Of how to take what life has dished you
and make the most of it,
With dignity.

Since my Mom's passing
I found a picture of my Mother, my sister, and me when my sister and I were teenagers.
And on the back of the picture she had written – it must have been many years ago because she could still write –
"Love this picture, Me and my gorgeous daughters, I can't see my writing. Forgive me."

"Forgive me."
That was my Mom.
A selfless woman who was always thinking of others
And who asked to be forgiven because *she* could not see as well as before
so that her writing was imperfect
Not an angry and bitter woman bemoaning her fate that her eyesight was failing.

If I could have one more conversation with my Mom, here is what I would say:

> "I love you Mom, I love you,
> each and every day.
> You were not a perfect Mom,
> You had your faults,
> But I loved you in every way.
> So, the gift of these years

that you spent in my hometown,
First in assisted living
And then in your own apartment with a live-in caregiver,
It was the gift of having lots of time together,
Time that we rarely seemed to have when I was a child
When you were a workaholic schoolteacher
Or you were focusing on my late wonderful father.

Mom, you were so beautiful

And you took such an interest in your appearance
That has always been a role model for me and
For so many others.
You taught me to put moisturizer on my face everyday
A routine that's helped me to have nice skin all these years.
And you taught me to take pride in the clothes I wear
Because you were such a stylish dresser.
And you taught me to take my own attractiveness in stride
Because you were so stunning and yet you were comfortable with your beauty.

You were a role model of physical fitness
Before it was a popular buzz word,
Biking, running, and then walking daily with
Dad well into your 70s.

And you were ahead of your time
In so many other ways
Because you were focused on your career,
Delegating housework,
And you were ordering take out before any
other families in Queens were doing that.
You were using frozen foods when others were
still cooking from scratch.
I grew up joking that my last name must have
been "Swanson"
Because we kids used to eat so many TV
dinners.

I know you bragged about me to my sister
And to your sister and to your friends
And I used to wish you had expressed your
appreciation of me more often directly to me
Although over the years you did put it in
writing, in cards and in letters
But over these last years together,
You learned to say it to me in person.
And I wrote it down on my iPhone whenever
you said it.
"You're terrific," you said so many times
And I have decided to dwell on those words
that you said,
Repeating those caring words in my mind,

Words I had waited so many years to hear directly from you.

And that is probably the greatest gift you have given me, Mom,
Because I saw you change so much over the years,
And so few are willing to work on themselves
But you were open to that.

Mom, I loved you,
And love you, and I will always love you.
And I respected you, and learned from you,
And I thank you for giving me life
And for being my mother
For life is the greatest gift you can give to anyone.

Thank you, Mom, for telling me how much my visits meant to you.
Thank you, Mom, for loving me.
Thank you, Mom, for our time together.
For having the courage at 79 to go to London with me to the London Book Fair
To help me with the booth for my publishing company
Even though you had never done anything like that before.

And thank you for the time we spent together in Chicago attending BookExpo.
Thank you for narrating my children's book, *The Cantaloupe Cat*.
And, when you were 87, thank you for going with me to the Broadway Show "Mary Poppins" even though you were already using a walker
And thank you for the trip to Florida to cousin Phyllis's son's wedding
As you charged through the new Jet Blue terminal at JFK,
pushing your walker in front of you
with such force, gusto, and determination.

And thank you for the time we went to meet actress Jane Seymour when they had a night in her honor at the Avon Theatre.

And thank you for going to the Passover Seder for women at the JCC.

And thank you for teaching me that if you have a job,
to throw myself into it 110% the way you did when you were one of the best kindergarten teachers anyone has ever seen.

And thank you for loving my late father for 54 years,
for showing me that a faithful, devoted, true love and marriage is possible

So, I fortunately found a love like that for my life in my husband and life partner Fred.

And thank you for showing me that a woman could have a family and a career.

And thank you for being a role model of making time for your friends as well as your family.

And thank you for being an example for so many of how you found love one more time after Dad died 16 years ago, with Dr. Bill, who passed away three years later,
and then your friendship with Larry Cohen nine years ago, who survives you.

And thank you for answering the questions I asked you when you first moved to Stamford
When your memory was sharper
So that I could get to know you better.

When I asked you for your favorite smells you told me it's "freshly baked chocolate chip cookies."

You told me your favorite memory is "eloping with Dad. Dad took his sneakers to pretend he was going to the gym but instead we went to the judge's chambers."

When you were a child, you said you wanted to be an actress when you grew up.

You shared that the novel you read that you most enjoyed was *Little Women*.

And when you were a child, you told me that you liked to play these sports: running and archery.

I felt love from you, Mom.
It might not have been the way I had once hoped I would feel love from my Mother
But the gift you gave me before you died
Is that I did – and do – feel that you loved and love me in your own way.
And the love you gave me is what I will keep in my heart forever.

So, my dear mother, this is my goodbye.

I will carry the many lessons you taught me and your love in my heart forever.

Rest in peace, my dear sweet Mom, rest in peace."

    There's another reason that my mother's passing inspired me to make it a priority to finally get this poetry collection published and available to you, my dear reader. My mother's death reminded me that since none of us have endless time, if I have a work or personal goal, I need to make it happen *now*. No more excuses. This poetry collection just had to get published whether it found a big audience or not. It is still the fulfillment of my commitment to myself to share a lifetime of poetry by Fred and by me.
    The majority of the 89 poems in this collection, are about love or work: romantic love, love of a child, grandchild, of a sibling, of a parent, of a friend, of places, even of a cat, and of nature. It's about love that is returned and love that is unrequited, and about "the single hours."

There are poems about work including Fred's time in Vietnam when he was in the Navy. Since Fred and I are both writers, you will find several poems in this book about writing, such as Fred's third poem in this collection, "Writing," which begins, "It is like sex." One of Fred's other poems related to work is what he witnessed when he was walking from the subway to his job in the World Financial Center, right near the Twin Towers, as the tragedy unfolded on September 11th, 2001. Although it's an essay, not a poem, I thought I should still include Fred's powerful reflection on that day that he wrote on the ten-year anniversary of the attacks.

I shared a poem I wrote recently about being an artist and what it was like to try to return to that skill after putting it aside for many years. Drawing on my work background in criminal justice, as well as my own life experiences as the younger sister of a homicide victim, I was moved to write a poem entitled, "The Victim," stirred by the untimely death of Reeva Steenkamp in South Africa by an international running celebrity.

How did Fred and I come up with the title, *In Love and Work*? We felt it would be very fitting to give this collection that title because when Fred answered the ad that I placed in the "personals" in *New York* magazine almost thirty years ago when I was searching for the love of my life, he put into his written reply that he was looking for a "collaborator in love and work."

That phrase—"in love and work"—has stayed with me and Fred and, over the years, we often restate it when we talk about our initial meeting as well as how our shared commitment to collaborating "in love and work" helps our relationship to grow and thrive. So it seemed only natural that our poetry collection would be called *In Love and Work*.

I encourage you to write your own poems, whether you publish those poems or you just write poetry for your own catharsis. Also reading poetry, whether it's contemporary or from the classical poets of the near or distant past, is another way to experience poetry, a form of writing I am pleased to say is having a revival of late.

I hope our poems inspire strong emotions in you whether it's laughter, sadness, empathy, or wonder as you visited with people and envisioned places that you have not been to before.

Most of all, let me end this note by letting you know that Fred and I celebrate each one of our readers. Thank you for taking the time to read this introduction and our collection of poetry.

Part One

by

Fred Yager

TODAY

You are my muse,
And my collaborator,
You are my fuse,
And my percolator.

In love and work,
We will create,
A world of wonder,
To help stimulate.

All those who
Come to hear us say,
Our love still grows
On Valentine's Day.

February 14, 2000

SEPTEMBER 11, 2001

I wonder when
I'll smile again.

Surrounded by
People in pain.

On the street,
Or on the train.

Where once was joy
Only sorrow remains.

Faraway stares
Of red rimmed eyes

So many tears
So many lives

Lost,
In a wasteful act
Of terror.

9/11 ... TEN YEARS AFTER: REFLECTIONS OF A SURVIVOR*

It's been 10 years since the planes came in and changed the landscape of lower Manhattan forever; 10 years since two commercial passenger airliners were turned into weapons of mass destruction by a small army of terrorists and flown into the North and South Towers of the World Trade Center. That attack on September 11, 2001 achieved what a truck bomb had failed to accomplish eight years earlier: the destruction of what some felt represented an architectural symbol of free market capitalism.

Anyone working in financial markets probably remembers where they were that day. I remember it as if it was yesterday. I was walking briskly across the Trade Center Plaza on my way to work when, at 8:45 a.m., I heard an explosion above my head. My first thought was that there was another bomb.

I looked up and saw a ball of fire and black smoke pouring out of a huge hole some 80 stories up the north side of the North Tower. Like most mornings, I was walking toward the bridge over West Street that connected the twin towers to the World Financial Center where I worked as a vice president of global broadcast services and president of Merrill Lynch Television.

I never made it to work that morning. And 10 years later, the images and feelings of that day remain branded in my mind and have haunted me since. Allow me to share some of them.

Before the fall

As I gazed up at the fireball and black smoke billowing from the side of the tower, it struck me that I should probably move. Pieces of burning debris were raining down around me. I made my way toward a crowd standing under the overhang of one of the smaller trade center buildings.

It was there that I found myself standing next to a middle-aged woman sobbing silently to herself and looking up. Before I could ask her what was wrong, I followed her line of sight to the ragged hole that had been torn from the building on the 86th floor.

Standing in the flaming opening was a man in a suit. He was adjusting his tie. And then he just leaned forward and fell from the gaping inferno.

He landed not far from where we were standing. The image of the man fixing his tie, weighing his options and then deciding to face fatal impact over death by fire is as clear today as it was a decade ago.

What kind of hell was behind him in that ragged hole that convinced him that falling 86 floors and certain death was the better alternative? What could he have been thinking? "This is my final journey so I should look good"?

I needed to make sense of what I had seen, to rationalize what could have motivated him to straighten his tie to be presentable when he entered the afterlife. Basically, I was frozen in place, unable to move, until another piece of smoking debris hit a few feet away and jarred me back to reality.

I looked at my watch and saw that it was almost 9 a.m. I was going to be late for work so I started walking again towards West Street and the World Financial Center. Along the way, I stopped a policeman and asked if he knew what had caused the explosion. He said he'd heard that a small plane had accidentally hit the North Tower and ordered me to keep walking because the area was no longer safe to stand.

A low-flying jet

Because of falling debris, the North Tower was closed, so I went down to street level to cross at Vesey Street. I was making my way toward West Street, keeping my eyes on the flaming tower, mostly worried about a shift in wind and how I would deal with that. Everywhere, people were stunned, dazed, crying and in shock. I felt like I was moving through a crowd of zombies who had just had the life sucked out of them

I just kept walking, hoping to make it to the office and sanity when I saw a jet plane flying down the Hudson River. It looked like it was flying pretty low and that seemed strange. The plane flew out over New York Harbor, towards the Statue of Liberty, then banked to the left and came around...

That's when the unbelievable happened. The plane leveled off and then flew right into the South Tower of the World Trade Center, ripping through the side of the building like a chainsaw, tearing out huge chunks of glass and masonry, and sending them sailing through the air. This was no accident. Two planes meant we were under attack. I started looking for shelter, as well as for more planes.

I didn't realize it at first, but a cloud of debris knocked loose from the South Tower was coming right toward me. I screamed: "Incoming! Incoming!" The stunned people nearby looked at me like I was crazy as I urged them to move and find shelter. This was no longer a safe place to stand. I ran until I was out of breath and then looked back. Now, both towers had raging gashes in their sides and balls of fire and black smoke billowing out of them.

A world on fire

I felt like I was back in Vietnam, in a firefight, wondering from which direction the enemy would strike next. I'd had nightmares like this. But this was no dream. This was real. In all my days in Vietnam, nothing was as bad as this. This was worse than war. This was hell and the world was on fire.

I tried calling the office, but no one was picking up the phone. I figured they must have evacuated the building. There was no way to get to the World Financial Center anymore anyway. Police were moving the crowds of people out of the area. I tried to call home but there was no longer any cell phone service. I couldn't tell anyone I knew that I was still alive.

Eventually, I made my way uptown to Broadway and 66th Street, where Merrill Lynch Television had a satellite office. A television was on and everyone was watching live coverage of the attack on the twin towers. I joined them, and we watched as the South Tower collapsed, followed a few minutes later by the North Tower.

A few hours later, I reached my frantic wife by phone and told her I was okay. In the days that followed, however, I realized I really wasn't okay. Emotionally and psychologically, I was wracked with guilt and horrific images that wouldn't go away. I felt guilty that I survived while so many around me died.

A loss

My company lost three people that day. I knew one of them and went to his memorial service. He was a young man in his mid-20's who worked in our department. He was engaged to be married, with his whole life ahead of him. He was the new guy in the office.

In Vietnam, it was always "the new guy" who got it – the new guy who didn't know how dangerous the terrain was. That day the new guy didn't know he could get killed just by having breakfast in the wrong restaurant 100 floors above Manhattan.

For months following the attack, every time I closed my eyes, I could see the ball of fire over my head and the businessman straightening his tie and then his body falling to earth.

Two months after 9/11, Merrill Lynch let us return to our offices in the World Financial Center. It was way too soon. The fires from the towers were still burning. The air had the odor of death and decay. Our desks were still covered with dust, and there were particles in the air. As I sat in my chair, I had the feeling I was surrounded by ghosts.

It's been ten years since I last walked across the Trade Center Plaza, past the giant metal globe glistening in the middle of a water fountain, where children would play and tourists would stop and take pictures. The plaza isn't there anymore. For many years, there was just a giant hole reminding us of the innocent and brave lives that were erased that day. It was like an open wound that wouldn't heal; a hole in the heart of a city in mourning.

Today, a new modern skyscraper is being erected in its place to both memorialize the spirits of nearly 2,700 souls who reside there and to show the world that life and commerce goes on, in a free-market world, even an economically challenged one.

TWENTY ONE YEARS

For twenty one years,
I've called you dear.

For twenty-one years,
You've allayed my fears.

For twenty one years,
We've shared our careers.

For twenty one years,
Our love knows no peers.

For twenty one years,
We laughed and shed tears.

For twenty one years,
You've lent me an ear.

For twenty one years,
You've made everything clear.

For twenty one years,
We blazed new frontiers.

For twenty one years,
You've given me reason to cheer.

For twenty one years,
You've been true and sincere.

For twenty one years,
It's been you I revere.

For twenty one years,
For you I cheer.

And for twenty one more,
I'll be first to volunteer.

Happy 21st wedding anniversary.

December 30, 2005

WRITING

It is like sex,
Sometimes like lovemaking,
Sometimes just hard pumping,
Sweat and firing off.

With a flick of our finger,
We turn on our typewriter.
You can feel its motor purr
As the inside warms up.

The keys, sensitive to the slightest touch,
Awaiting penetration of fingers and thought,
That grow into adult-like works,
Of poetry and prose.

When the act of writing is over,
There's a coming down,
A slowing of the pulse,
A softer breath as ideas,
Like sperm, are spent.
Sometimes missing, sometimes connecting.

Sometimes writing is like sex without passion,
When it feels more like typing, a going through the motions,
Rushing by rote toward an empty climax.

But when writing is like love,
The words gush out in torrents, full of
emotion, connecting, forming, creating,
Building a work that glows and lives on
Beyond the page.

HOTELS

Hotels can be lonely places
funeral homes for drifters.
Sad eyed hallways with lonely faces
Doormen that call you mister.
Little rooms all cold and damp
with chains across the doors
to keep the thieves out in the hall
and you inside to watch the wall.

THE BALLAD OF EVIL ELY

A windy sunset paints a pale yellow sky,
a dusty haze rolls over the land now dry
a lone tired rider tries hard not to die
on his low backed mare,
blind in one eye.

From Phoenix he rode a new job to try
Down Tombstone way where the dead men lie
shot down by the wicked outlaw, Evil Ely
who makes women beg
and little children cry.

A hundred dollars in gold was the price on his head
a hundred dollars in gold, either alive or dead,
a hundred dollars in gold but little was said,
till the lone rider came to town,
needing money for bread.

Tombstone was quiet when he came that day
the stranger so weary on his broken down bay
but he needed that gold for his debts to pay
Ely cried out, "Stop," and the stranger's
face turned gray.

The stranger's eyes watered as the sun beat down cruel
Ely walked into the street, strong, sturdy and cool,
That's when the stranger knew that this man was no fool
And for Evil Ely or the stranger,
It would be the last duel.

Heads filled all the windows

Wondering eyes peered from the doors
Merchants gathered their goods
and closed down their stores.
The townsfolk said a prayer
and hoped the stranger would score
then the stranger drew and fired
but dust had filled his bore.

His gun exploded in his hand
As half his body covered with blood
as he fell to the sand.
the stranger cried out with pain
and the people lost hope for peace in their land.
The stranger squirmed in the street
Ely walking over, laughing,
firing hot lead at his feet.

Then he bent over the stranger
to put an end to his life
But when Ely bent over,
the stranger pulled out a knife.

Ely just laughed and cocked his colt
As the stranger lunged and caught Eli's throat.
But his gun went off,
And the stranger fell back,
Ely looked around,
blood squirting from his neck.

He knew he was dying,
the stranger was dead
he began seeing spots,
lights flashed in his head.

His stomach was empty and wanted to be feed,
His body was tired, and needed a bed.

People began circling the two bodies in the street
but jumped back when Ely tried to speak.
And before Ely died, his head he did turn
as he said,
"Bury him good with the money he earned."

A SECRET BIRTHDAY POEM

Here are a few short words,
To wish you well,
On your 56th birthday,
But who could tell?

You look 20 years younger
With a smile so bright,
I can't wait to see you,
When we're alone tonight.

Then we'll celebrate proper,
Like all lovers should.
I hope you like to be ravished
Because I know I would.

So have a happy birthday
And a wonderful night.
I love you forever,
And it feels so right.

December 16, 2004

A COLD DAY IN DECEMBER

This is a day to celebrate our love,
A love that began over 22 years ago,
On a cold day in December,
On a day your knees buckled
And my heart skipped a beat.

Through thick and thin,
For richer and poorer,
In sickness and in health
Our love still grows,
In a marriage that's never been dull.

Collaborating again
In love and work,
My freelance companion
From morning to night,
From breakfast to bed.

You're in my heart
You're in my head
I just need on more line

Love you forever, Fred

February 14, 2006

ANOTHER YEAR FLIES BY

Another year flies by,
Life with you is never dull.
A promise made by you,
And you came through.

I may not have money
For silver hearts with inscriptions,
But I'll give you my soul,
And dedicate all my transcriptions.

Sometimes words are all I can afford.
You know I'd spend more if I could.
But then sometimes words are worth more
Than all the money in the world.

I'm not jealous of your women friends,
You deserve them.
I know I can't fill all your needs,
And that's all right.

You're still my best friend,
And I treasure every day with you.
You've made a tough year tender,
You've made every day one to remember.

So on this day of your birth,
Some 54 years before,
We'll celebrate your life,
We couldn't ask for more.

December 16, 2002

ALL YOU ARE

All that my heart touches,
All that my soul endures,
All that ever matters,
All that's mine is yours.

All the times we traveled
To places near and far,
To me you are my everything,
All that is, all you are.

January 5, 2001

BEACH FORTRESS

A white-capped princess lives in a castle of white sand,
Formed from the heart of a young man's hand.
The beautiful princess,
She's the love of the land.

The small lad has built a sturdy beach fortress,
Strong enough to protect its tiny peace princess.
With towers that touch the sky,
Walls packed thick and high,
And a moat to keep out
Witches, warlocks and unwanted passersby.

The princess will reign in the castle's sun,
The children will sing and dance and run,
Happiness is loving till the day is done,
When the tide comes in
and washes out all the fun.

ONE NIGHT IN GOLDEN GATE PARK

We lay on a grassy bank bed,
Near the Swan Pond in the park.
The night wind warm,
It's breeze like the breath of God,
As we made life-giving love,
Under a blanket of fog.

We hit liquid state when the nightmare came,
Sounding like two thousand motorcycles
Riveting and roaring just beyond the wall of white,
Breaking the panting, sighing silence.

We must have looked like
Two naked angels in hell,
Enhanced in exhaust,
Embracing, entangled, wearing
Nothing but each other's smile.

Like ghost riders in the night,
A dozen bikers crashed through
the fog and formed a circle
around us.
Nothing brings love closer than fear.

Our decision came mutually,
That if this was how it would all
end, so be it.
Ignoring the obvious danger,
Denying the potential.

We continued to move together,
Performing now for our new
found fans.

But then a miracle happened.
The fog began to lift,
The bikers raised up their
thumbs and then rode off in the
night.

We watched them ride away,
Then turned to find each other's
thoughts.
No big deal, we agreed.
Probably happens all the time.

A QUIET DAY

It was just a quiet day,
Of back ally Frisbee,
Beer and chin bowling,
Sandwiches and soup.

I didn't know you were
A cracker connoisseur.
Want to play a game
Of hearts to a hundred.
Penny a point.
Winner buys donuts
In the morning.

The sun's gone down.
Street lights on.
We sat on soft pillows
And cuddled till dawn.

In the window we sat,
Trading gazes eye for eye,
Until the cat got caught
In the carpet
And begged for help.

Can I be your savior too?

SILENT SHOWER

Feel the rain moving in.
Leaves roll over
in their branch beds,
Tucked in by a damp cooling wind.

A black and white striped spider
Jerks nervously across the pavement.
A mantis prays and gets lost in the lawn.
The sun winks, then blinks,
As an eyelid cloud closes.
Gray from horizon to horizon.

A lonely sparrow perched on a pole,
Notices the change, whistles a wish,
And flies off to where ever birds go
when it rains.

Suddenly, the first drop is fired.
A direct hit!
An ant scrambles for a crack.
A dog shaking and spraying,
hunches soggy toward a tree,
To wait out the rain.

A silent shower, then the sun.
Over as soon as it had begun.
The sparrow chirps,
The ant smiles.
The cement sidewalk glistens bright,
Then dries.

HALF KIDS

As I stood at the landing,
Heavy metal feedback,
Ringing in my ears,
I remembered how
The cabaret used to be
Before they came,
The half kids,
With their pissed-off,
Punk filled world.

It was warm here once,
before the half kids came.
Music would float in the air,
With melodies so thick you could feel them,
Lyrics so clear you could understand them.
Now, the most popular song is
The whipping-whooping wail of a police siren.

They strolled in by the hundreds,
The half kids,
Trying so hard to look tough.
Trying so hard to look different,
But all wearing the same stray cat look.
Lost and alone, together.

They stray in and stay
Till it gets cold or they get hungry.
It's what's happening
And everyone seems to know why
Except the poor half kids,
Who end up making love sadder
Than it already is sometimes.

Their bodies pierced and tattooed,
Their fantasies black and blue.
I studied the half kid style,
And realized they never smile.
It must be hard being a half kid.
But then, weren't we all one once?

LONESOME ROADS

We all walk alone,
On lonesome roads,
Along rivers of the heart.

Wrestling within
Our desperate selves
To touch another soul.

Then we disconnect
To reclaim memories
From another place and time.

Down alleys and valleys
searching,
for something lost,
but not forgotten.

Faded images of
friends and lovers
Of life disappearing.

It's as if the ghosts of yesterday
Had the answer to today.

TWO SIDES OF THE RAINBOW

It's a gray mid afternoon,
In a slow Sunday shower.
People walk along hunched over and dripping.

Bushes glisten,
As tree squirrels listen
to the leaves
plop, plopping.
Sleepy rain drops dropping,
turning the grass ground
into a sponge.

The council of generals
were stranded at the eighteenth hole,
Seeking shelter under the flag.

"It's sabotage, I tell ya," said the commandant.
"Happens every time I golf, and every time I want."

"I've just been hit," cried the Secretary of Defense.
"It's a neck wound, and it's dripping.
"Get the towel doc."

The chief of staff took off and all dismayed
but soon he did return with towels
somewhat frayed.

"We'll fight to the drench," they all agreed.
"We'll go down in history,
With Palmer, Player, and Sneed."

"We can't give up the green,"

They battle cried.
"We'll maintain hole eighteen."
Then the sun came out and sighed.

Nearby, a farmer walked out to his fields,
where his crops had almost died.
He looked up to see a rainbow,
Then looked down and almost cried.

ANOTHER NIGHT OF DRINKING IN A DUSTY TEXAS TOWN

Crazy Dan's sitting in the corner,
His dog drunk by his side,
He just ran Wild Henry out of town,
And he's feeling satisfied.

The pool balls are a crackin',
And the money's gonna fall,
To the one who makes the shot,
And sinks that old eight ball.

Just another night of drinking
In a dusty Texas town.
Just another night of drinking,
Just another king to crown.

For years they came
and for years they went.
Strangers from other towns,
Money bet and money spent.

They'd challenge Dan the king,
They hustled all night,
Some went home busted,
Some put up a fight.

That's when Crazy Dan
Would leave his corner,
Armed with his stick,
Make some wife a mourner.

Today, the corner's empty,

Henry's sister came to town
Found Crazy Dan and his dog
And shot the two fools down.

The pool tables are all quiet,
The sharks are passing through
and everyone's afraid to shoot,
They shot, they learned, they knew.

Just another night of drinking
In a dusty Texas town.
Just another night of drinking,
Just another king to crown.

VIETNAM*

There's a still wind blowing,
Through the trees in Vietnam,
Passing leaves not turning,
It comes from houses burning,
And carrying the scent of dying.
There's no more people crying,
They were silenced by a bomb.

You can't throw a ball
That's already tossed.
We can't win a war
That's already lost.

We'd sit in Saigon balconies,
Drinking beer and watching the war go rotten.
In Washington they drank scotch
and with each sip, the war was forgotten.

Far from you, I'd lay,
Calling out your name.
Back in the barracks,
Bottom bunk,
I'd walk you through wires,
And bring you through springs,
Kiss you good night at sheet's edge.

Tomorrow hours closer,
The week ends for you.

*These three additional poems by Fred Yager about Vietnam are included in the collection, *The Healing Power of Creative Mourning: Poems* (Hannacroix Creek Books, Inc., 2000): "Silenced by a Bomb," "Cold Day in Summer," and "We Won't Go."

The tour gets shorter with every breath.

My pillow protects me
While I'm away.
Its fluff is enough for now.

But nothing will ever replace
Your softness
Or the way you feel in the morning.

SAN FRANCISCO, SUMMER OF '67

It rains a lot in San Francisco.
Unexpectedly, without warning,
Clouds leap out over the hills
to trap you.

They'll even wait till you're out
on the street,
Going to a movie, or to see a friend.
You can't escape the rain.

Awnings on the stores of Chinatown
offer some protection,
But they tend to be full of holes.
Even the best built homes have faults.

For a while I shared an apartment
on Grant Avenue in Chinatown
over a catering service and movie theater,
across the street from Jack's Restaurant and Fish
Market.

"Look at the fish in the tank,
They're alive," said a tourist in passing.
"It ain't the fish that's alive lady,
It's the water," said a young man on acid.

Our door was always open,
Neighborhood kids would come over
to play their games of war.
The place always looked like a battlefield.

"Bombs away. Rat a tat tat."

"You're dead."
"Am not."
"I just blew you up."
"Oh yeah? I poisoned your peanut butter."
"Not fair. Only conventional warfare."

War is for kids.

From a Golden Gate sunset,
to a Chinatown masquerade,
on down,
and around,
steep redbrick turns of Lombard,
to the Market Street protest parade.

Don't care much for the Fairmont.
But God save the Mark!
I'll chase you through Ashbury
and let the pigeons guard the park.

If time had a trading post
where you could exchange your life,
To make the most
on that counter my past I'd throw
just to spend another day
in San Francisco.

I'VE JUST BEEN WONDERING

Nothing Dad, nothing Mom.
I've just been wondering,
That's all.

What's it all about?
This life thing.

Is it because
or is it just that way?
Or could it just have happened?
Or was it always this way?
That's all.

I'll understand if you don't know.

SOLITARY CONFINEMENT

On the verge of tears,
Near the edge of sorrow,
I find a familiar anguish,
As the friendly pain
Of living alone fills every moment.

In the years we shared,
You taught me how to live,
But now you're gone
And my world holds no tomorrows.

I search for you in dreams,
But you're never there.
Emptiness rises up from deep sleep,
Sucking all life from my heart.

When love dies,
There must be punishment.
The sentence, solitary confinement.

OVEREXPOSED: A DREAM

There's a latent image forming,
On the emulsion of my mind.
An exposure timed for settings,
Only fast films rarely find.

It blurred at first, but settled clear,
An inch from my opened eye.
A few molds of flesh formed for an ear,
Beneath hair the color of rye.

No breath seeped from this female form,
Pressed to me like a suit.
No pulsing heart for a body warm,
But skin as cold as morning fruit.

An instant passed when memory flashed,
To what happened the night before.
Rolling and rolling until we crashed,
Throwing us out the driver's side door.

Too many drinks were the cause of it all.
Too much of the merry life.
Why couldn't that fatal axle fall
on me instead of my wife?

WINTER DREAMS

With the summer came the sand and sea,
Beaches, baseball, and winter dreams.
That summer brought you close to me,
Now far away, or so it seems.

You purred like a cat
That gets stiff backed and arched.
You with your hat,
That can be washed, ironed and starched.

I'd say something funny,
You'd spray mouthfuls of wine.
I'd pretend not to know you
And you'd be especially kind.

And we'd walk along gazing,
At the flat world of the sea.
A wave in,
A wave rolled out
A fisherman strikes
And explains with a shout.

"It's a dandy fish,
But I've caught bigger.
It fought to its death.
But not as well as I figured."

Men of war lay baking on the shore.
A lonely surfer hustles,
Has to catch one more.
Walking and talking,
We'd make lists of our poets.

Sharing every other line,
Criticizing great artists saying,
"You should see one of mine."

We'd talk of economics,
For what it's worth.
Relating pediatrics
And the miracle of birth.

Strolling on to sunset,
Knowing night's end.
Then, in an affectionate delay,
You'd lower your head
And seriously say,
"This is the last time for us.
 It will all be past present,
 When I climb on that bus."

So we wished each other luck.
You'd say "I hope you do what you want to do."
And I'd say, "Me too you."

We'd look at each other for words,
But there's nothing left to say.
Your mouth smiled, while your sad eyes cried.
You climbed on the bus, I walked to my car.
The flower you put over the dashboard had died.

Padre Island, Texas, 1968

THE FIRE NEXT TIME

The fire was going out,
A fire that took so long
In igniting.
It had to get really hot,
Before it burned.

Hard wood has a high kindling point,
And as hard as it was to start,
It was just as hard to put out.

So in the slow burn,
Of a dying flame,
A few tears fell,
And the fire
Flickered and died.

Dead but still smoldering,
I scraped away some ash.
Beneath what had burned
was more hard wood.
Charred, but able to burn again.

And it will burn again,
But as its nature,
The fire next time
Will have to be much hotter.

IT SCARES ME

Why am I blocking
how my heart screams for you?

It scares me how,
The pain in me,
Felt the pain in you.
How it clawed at my chest,
How my head ached with sorrow.

You are leaving,
And we haven't even met.

It scares me how
I can feel the pull around your eyes,
Dams holding back oceans of tears,
From years of sadness
That would make the whole world moan,
And send the nighttime weeping.

It scares me how
An empty me could feel an empty you.
And like a breeze that causes a flame to flare,
You swept past the coals of my soul
And burned what remained of my heart.

BLUE WHITE

It's all blue white, very bright,
The day has just begun.
My mind is weary, muscles tight,
My time is almost done.

Blue white is getting brighter,
The midday sun is finally here,
My heart is getting lighter.
The end is drawing near.

Blue white is getting dimmer now,
The night has finally come.
I'm probably dead,
But it's been said,
Life has really, just begun.

FRACTURED

Someday there'll be a clothes shop for cripples.
Fashions for fractures.
Casts that match cumber buns.
Multicolored crutches that phos-phoresce.

They say that clothes make the man.
But what about the wounded soldiers and sportsmen
who wear the trophies of torture?
Or are broken bones simply out this year?

Someone should open a lounge for limpers,
A salon for the gimpers.
I just hope it happens soon.
I've got three more weeks in a golden foot cast.

JUST AIN'T AROUND ANYMORE

My friend Barry Baist,
Is going to waste,
With his perverted taste,
And an addiction to paste,
Looks for things to embrace,
Lives in gray states of grace,
Never could find his place
Just ain't around any more.

My friend William Kidd,
Just opened a lid,
Never here, always hid,
Has fond thoughts of the grid,
And is now up for bid,
Time trials the fid,
Reads the Wizard of Id,
Just ain't around anymore.

My friend Texas Pete,
Who thinks so neat,
Always doing great feats,
Goes for walks in bare feet, and so modestly greets,
Older women in heat,
On one way streets,
Just ain't around any more.

My friend Senator Gray has nothing to say,
Looks for needles in hay,
Doesn't know how to play,
Walks roads going no way,
Then gets lost far away,
After going astray,
Just ain't around anymore.

WE KNEW

The same places and faces,
Don't know what to do.
All ideas my mind erases,
My thoughts are of you.

Nothing will ever come of us,
This we both know.
Our dreams have all turned to dust,
And soon I will go.

We'll then just be memories,
To remember and tell.
To our friends, maybe enemies,
That we knew each other well.

RUNNING AWAY

I started running away
As soon as I could walk.
Tiny footprints in the snow
Were my good-byes.

I remember the taste
Of bitter snowflakes on my tongue,
And the creak of rusted buckles
On old galoshes.

I remember wondering,
Would they try to find me?
Would they even care
That I was gone?

Most of all,
I remember the pain,
Frozen in my heart,
like frostbite on my soul.

Too young to understand,
Too afraid to question why,
I just knew then,
That I had to run away.

Today, years later,
I'm much wiser and
Full of understanding.
But I still feel like running away,

I FOUND YOU

I find I've finally found you,
I want you to know,
How much I want you,
And want you to want
The love I have for you.

A simple love,
Like yours and mine,
A quiet love of truth and time.
I want the world to know
We're two of a kind.

We'll shout it out and make it known,
We're together forever, never alone.

Someday I'll take the time
To write a song for you.
A melody to show you how I feel
And what I'm going through.

A simple tune with the words
I want to say
That you mean more to me now
Than you did yesterday.

Like a flower about to bloom,
A fresh face in a crowded room,
Embracing life, so full of fun,
You became a woman on the run.

But still, I find I've finally found you.
Why were you hiding so hard?

SO CAN I

Watched by day,
Touched by sight,
Licked by sound,
Swallowed in scent.
I am an island.

Decision, decisions,
There's so many ways to look.

Tidal waves of pain,
Breaking,
Smoothes my sand
Into a beach of joy.

Falls the water
Spraying mist whitely
Over sculptured rock
Chiseled by the foam.

       Grass does grow
       So can I.

LONELY EYES

She had the loneliest eyes.
    I can tell lonely eyes
        I've seen my own reflections many lonely times.

It's a far away look
    As if you don't belong there or anywhere.

How beautifully ugly loneliness can be.
    The loneliness being ugly
    The emptiness in all its beauty.

Thoughts usually come hard during emptiness.

But once you're completely empty
    Entirely alone
    Once you cross the line
    Into the quiet world
They return…crystal clear.

MEDITATION

Keep your wits, she said,
You gotta keep your wits.
'Cause if you lose control
The world spins on and you get left behind.
Left behind and helpless,
A sad place to be lonely.

All is clear.
The questions are the answers.
The truth never hurts as much as the lie.
My mind goes in circles.
I feel the things I'm thinking now
I've thought before, and before,
And I'll probably think them again
Only now the circle is wider,
The thoughts deeper.
Cluttered with a past,
Meditation is like a broom
Sweeping up a messy mind.

WITH CHILD

For Lupe

You'll be a mother soon,
carrying with you a beginning.
Just a belly full of love now,
An inner warmth,
A heater for the heart,
A baby's being born.

Your young mother's mind is mixing a million names,
One for he, one for she,
Not knowing, not really caring what will be.

You wear the sign of love,
Working a miracle with every breath.
The world and I
Have never loved you more
For you've just been touched by God.

I'VE GOT A SONG

I've got a song for Simon
I've got a song for Paul
It's the same song for Peter
It even fits us all.

It's the song of life
It's the song of love
It's the song of giving
Sung from above.

It's a song for believers
And agnostics too
For they are believers
In what they do.

It's a song for changing
The times that must
A song for arranging a world of trust.

It's a song for all people
To live hand in hand
To God, we're just one color
That color is man.

TO BE UNDERSTOOD

To read
    Or to be read.
That is the question.

To read and understand
    May be Christ-like
    But to write and be understood
    Is God-like.

BRINGING LOVE CLOSE

We lay open
on a grassy bank bed
near the swan pond
might wind warm
the breeze like the breath of God
as we made life-giving love
under a blanket of stars.

We hit liquid state
alas two thousand motorcycles
riveting roaring
broke the painting sighting silence.

Like two angels in hell
enhanced in exhaust
embracing, wearing each other
mothing brings love close faster than fear.

They drove by waving
thumbs up approval
as we watched them ride away,
Then turned to find each other's thoughts.

No big thing,
we agreed,
happens all the time.

THE LISTENER

The Listener is precious,
Overworked, underpaid,
He too would be a talker
But too often, he's afraid.

So he remains content to listen,
To hear the tales we spin.
So do the listener a favor,
When you talk, say something.

HAPPY VALENTINE'S DAY

Valentine's Day without you here
Isn't the same as when you're near.

To feel your body next to mine,
On this celebration of love so fine.

Today's Thursday is just another day
With the love of my life so far away.

The hours drag on until my morning flight
I wonder just how I'll get through the night
knowing that tomorrow brings me home,
And that we are both determined that somehow
this is the last time we'll ever be alone.

February 14, 2013

Forty-one Years,

It seems like yesterday when I first saw your face
Your smile could light up every room in the place.

It's been forty-one years, and I'll take 41 more
Forty-one years, but who's keeping score?

We've shared a lifetime of living and loving
You promised me that it would never get boring.

Forty-one years, they flew by so fast
Some of them said it would never last.

But we beat the odds when we met that day
Forty-one years ago, and it's like yesterday.

We've spent more than half of our lives together
Raised two sons, with families, we treasure

Forty-one years of working side by side.
Forty-one years of sheer joy and pride.

We've paved the way for more of the same
A future together, both sharing one aim

Living a life well-lived, it's how you win this game

Happy 41st Anniversary, my dear darling Jan.

Thank you for sharing this life, your number one fan.

December 30, 2025

Part Two

by

Jan Yager

WRITING IN A FISH BOWL

I, who thought I needed quiet,
And to be alone,
Find I can write
And push our babe in a swing,
While my husband writes
Or talks on the phone.

A minute here,
An hour there,
Never more than one or two.
That's the consequence
Of having found a mate,
And being not one,
But two, now three.

Our son's needs come first
For at five months
His appreciation of the literary
Is less than his thirst.

This fish bowl life is fine for some
I had enough of the other one.
The hours, days, and weeks
Of uninterrupted time,
To write, compose, rewrite, and wish.

While our son naps
On the computer I can quietly compose
Not as much as before, I confess,
But my life is fuller now,
More, not less.

February 1985

FEBRUARY 14TH

Today is a day
Not like any other day.
Today is the day
That lovers say
"Happy Valentine's Day."

But for me
Every day is a loving day
With you because
For me
Every moment we share
Is my wildest dreams come true.

I love you, sweet Fred,
I adore you with all my heart.
You are my hero
You are my favorite writer
You are so passionate
So sensitive
So insightful.

I rejoice in the years together
And look forward to the ones ahead.

Thank you for being my Valentine, dear Fred,
Thank you for sharing my life,
My heart,
My fantasies,
My thoughts,
My wishes,
My bed.

SLIPPING AWAY

Slipping away,
More each day,
Mom, you are just slipping away,
What more can I say?

We had a really nice visit with extended family
in April
At least there was some recognition and discussion,
But during the next visit or two with just me
I saw that a dramatic change had taken place.

I didn't know it was going to happen
Or I would have prepared for it,
I would have planned for it.

There were so many questions I still wanted to ask
you:
What was it like being apart from Daddy during World
War II?
Did you still harbor any negative feelings toward the
Germans or the Japanese?

Are you glad you retired at 64?
Would you have done any things differently?
How do you manage to be so pleasant and positive
despite your dementia?

What was my grandfather like?
All I know is that he died at 49
And that he was a wonderful man
But what does that *really* mean?

What's your favorite memory of your father?
How can I, even now, learn more about my grandfather
through your faded memories?
What about my grandmother?
There are the stories I've heard over the years
But what about the day-to-day grandmother, your
mother, when she was young?

Yes, I can still ask my Mom those questions
But now, since the sudden change occurred,
Mom just can't answer me.
And it's sad
So very sad
It makes me cry inside in a deep empathetic way
That is so powerful and overwhelming.

The connection I feel with my sons
And my husband
And my sister
And some of my other relatives
and a few of my friends whom I really care about
in that deep way that whatever happens to any of these
people it's as if it happened to me.

I now *finally* feel that empathy with my Mother
Now, finally, after all these years.
She's 89 now
And it isn't too late because she's still here
But she's not able to remember or speak very much
anymore
And it's so very sad
And humbling
As I make a stronger commitment
To write more down

To ask everyone I love more questions
Before it's too late
Because those memories should be part of our present
And our future
And that's only possible if we share those memories.

May 2011

ON OUR FIFTH ANNIVERSARY

These last five years
are the best I've known.

These last five years
How our love and
our family has grown.

I look to the next fifty
with you by my side.

I look to the future with you
Taking the ups and downs in stride.

I'd marry you again in an instant
For once in a lifetime a choice that's right occurs

I love you, dear,
And even if it's been said before
I love you each year,
More and more.

December 30, 1989

THE SURPRISE

We had to take two cabs
There were too many of us with our two kids and
Their friends
But we rushed for that train.

You didn't think we'd make it
But we made it in time
For the next express,
Since there would not be another express for an hour.

So we looked for you and the boys
Waiting on the platform
Expecting you all to come racing toward the train
And then we'd all jump on together.

But when you called on your cell phone and said,
"Where are you?"
And I realized that you had left on that train without me
My heart sank down to my toes.

I was shocked, stunned, and surprised that you didn't wait
That you didn't make sure
That I was also on the train.

I felt alone
Abandoned
Sad.

Was that an overreaction?
Yes.

Were the feelings real?
Yes.

I cried. I said expletives, uncouth words.
I know it wasn't just the train.
I know it wasn't just you.
It was something deeper,
Something from my earliest years.
The feeling of being abandoned.
The feeling of being left behind.
Worst of all, the fear that we were not connecting.

But then I called when we finally made the third train,
I called and figured, by now, you were already at home.

But no!
My hero
My prince
my best friend
my lover
You were still at the train station!

Exhausted, you were there,
waiting for me
Waiting to make sure I arrived safely
and got to my car safely.

And I felt the joy of being loved and cared for that is so special
    so wonderful
        so completely fulfilling.

Seeing you at the train station

It was like the first time I saw you at
That bar where we met
After I called you
After you answered my ad in the personals.

It was purely an emotional reaction
This feeling that "I love this man.
I like this man,
I want to spend my life with this man."

This man, my dearest Fred,
This man was, and still is, you.

YOUR VALENTINE'S DAY GIFT TO ME

You could have gotten me diamonds,
After all, diamonds are forever.

And you've gotten me diamonds before
And I cherish each and every one,
No matter how big,
No matter how small.

You could have gotten me a book
And that would have been okay too
Because books have always been my friend
And I write books
And I read books
And I cherish books and words and ideas.

You could have gotten me a negligee
As you've done before
And I like to wear those naughty nighties
Because it's fun
but fortunately
You don't *need* me to wear those naughty nighties.
Just being me is enough.

And it feels so good to finally
Be "enough" for someone
And I love you for that.

You could have gotten me chocolates
Now that I'm thin again
And I wouldn't have seen any hidden
Messages in the gift of chocolates
Any criticisms

Any innuendoes
And I could have had one or two or more
Chocolates
And enjoyed each bite
And not felt guilty
Finally
Because chocolate is good
Chocolate is delicious
As long as I stay in control
And eat just enough.

But instead you got me something that
Does not last
Something that is of the moment
A bouquet of flowers
Roses so red
And leaves so green
The colors filled the dining room
And then in every room that I moved those flowers to
for the week that the roses lasted.

I saved the glass bowl
And that will be forever
But the flowers didn't last
At least not in a real way.

But those flowers will last forever in my heart
As surely as if those flowers were diamonds
Or a negligee
Or a book.

Those flowers were the purchase of an impulsive man
A man who put love before reason
A man who threw caution to the wind and spent

A lot, too much, on a bouquet that would not last very long.

I know.
I found the receipt the other day.
And I gasped when I saw how much those flowers cost.
And I remembered what you said.
That it was the only bouquet left and the clerk told you the price
But you took the flowers anyway.

A luxury, yes, a luxury.

So I want you to know that the money you spent was not wasted.
Yes, I know there are those starving around the world and I *do* care about them
And I'm trying to make it a better world without starvation, without poverty
But for one moment I was indulged.
I was indulged with an outrageously expensive bouquet for Valentine's Day.

And I love you for indulging me
And I thank you for it.
I will savor the feeling forever.

HAPPY FATHER'S DAY, DADDY, UP IN HEAVEN

I think of you a lot, you know,
Not just on special days.
But today is "your day"
And I miss you so.

Your grandsons have grown so much
Since you saw them last.
Scott's going on twenty,
Jeff's going on sixteen.
They were just ten and six when you
Went to Heaven.

On this, your day, I want to tell you
We are fine, but it's not the same without you.
But I will try to dwell on the joyful memories we had,
Dad, like the family trip to the Catskills when I was ten.

Or the two years at our summer home in Greenwood Lake
Or when you drove to where I was teaching to drive me back to my apartment
Even though it took more than 2 hours once a week
Because I was pregnant with my son Scott
And I didn't' have a car ride home from the college
On Long Island where I was an assistant professor.

Then we would try to have lunch when we got to Manhattan
But it was strained as we searched for things to say.

I wish I had more time with you so we could have reduced that strain.
I think we could have if we had more time.

I have a great phone relationship with Mom
But the strain is there with her
when we get together in person.

I have the time to try to reduce the strain when Mom and I get together
But I don't go to visit Mom enough, just Mom and me.

On this Father's Day I will make you and me a promise, Dad,
I will try harder to forge a relationship with Mom that won't have any regrets.
Because I still have a chance with Mom on earth
And I know from losing you that the chance can be a fleeting thing
And I don't want any regrets again.

I hope you're having a nice Father's Day in Heaven.
Do they serve a special brunch for the Dads and Grandads today?
Do you get together with your friends Lil and Dave
Who joined you in the last year or so?

We're taking your son-in-law Fred out for brunch today
We'll be giving him presents and cards.

I'm not sure if Mom will be with her friend Larry and his sons today
Or if Larry will be with them without Mom.

I'll call her and find out.
I'll read her this poem.

We all want you to know that we remember you
Everyday but especially today.

Bye for now, wonderful Father.
I was always proud that you were my father.

I think you were proud of me as your daughter.
Sometimes I reread your letters to me that I saved over the years
It was before e-mail
So you would write letters when I was away.

I must try to send letters and cards to my children now and then,
Not just e-mails,
Because letters are special
And you can save letters and cards.

Love,
Your daughter Jan

June 29, 2005

MY NEW FRIEND

A special friend called me today,
And, for once, she talked, I listened,
And, this time, she took, I gave.

My life turned around today as I realized
That I'll be okay
So I can give, and not always take.

My friend shared with me
Her life, her thoughts, her fears.
I'll bet my friend has waited to be able
To share with me for these decades of years.

For today she became my friend
As well as my mother.

MOMISMS

I've heard that those with Alzheimer's may become
Different than they used to be.
Someone who was sweet can turn vicious
And someone who was nasty may become sweet.

There's a difference of opinion over whether the
"new" personality is the "real" one
Hiding underneath the other persona
All those years.

I guess you would believe that depending upon
Whether your loved one became the "nice" or
The "nasty" person once the dementia took hold.

In your case, dear Mom, you became so very nice
As if that's the Mom you were always meant to be.
My sister bears witness to this
But during our formative years
You sometimes said things that we knew you didn't mean.
You sometimes called us names or labeled us
In unflattering and even cruel ways.

We never knew why you did that
Because most of the time you were so nice
Especially to others
To our father and to your friends
But we still loved you
Because you were our Mom
Despite those negative words or comments
That hurt our feelings

We would not and could not stop loving you.

So you can imagine
What a delightful surprise it was for me
To find that dementia caused you to
Say some of the wonderful things to me
That I had dreamed you would one day say.

I decided that I could not let those opportunities go by,
I just had to mark those words,
To write down those positive words,
So I could reread those words,
To try to cancel out the negative words
That, till that point, were much more characteristic
Of what I remembered you saying to me.

And so I began the habit of using my iPhone
To write down something I began to call a
"Momism."
And here are some of those "Momisms" that I thank
you for because this is what I will read
And reread always:
"I'm so glad you're here" you said to me just a month
ago, only a few weeks before you died.

Or when I asked you, three years ago,
"Mom, what are your thoughts today?"
And you answered, "That I love you more than ever."

Or when you shared with me, just a few days later,
This declaration about yourself:
"I have a wonderful family."

Or when you said to me, a year later,

"You're looking wonderful, gorgeous."

Or five days later when you said,
"Gee I love this visit."

Why are these Momisms so important?
Because I tried to do business with a woman for five
months who had never heard a positive "Momism"
from her mother.
I spent countless hours with this intelligent woman
every week, working on projects with her,
Talking to her,
And it was a very tough time for me
But I was willing to get through it
Despite the way she treated me
Because I am a professional
And I wanted us to have the shared benefits
Of making those projects happen,
And I knew it was her pain that caused her to be
Such a difficult person to work with.
I initially even wanted to be her friend
As well as her colleague.
I even set her up on a blind date
With someone I thought she might find
Romance with because she seemed so lonely
And that single friend was such a
Nice guy, I thought they'd make a match.
But that didn't work out
And I soon realized that it was very unlikely
That she and I could be friends
Since her unfounded contempt for me
Kept growing.
The more I put up with her behavior
Because I still saw a caring person

Underneath all the venom
The more she seemed to detest me for still
Liking her.

But I was willing to keep working on forging a
positive working relationship with her
But it soon became apparent that even that would not
happen
Probably because her mother never gave her the love
she needed
And even on her death bed, her mother couldn't
Tell her that she loved my colleague.
This narcissistic woman seemed never to have heard
even one kind "Momism."
This woman was tortured by that
And she ended our relationship abruptly in a way
That hurt me professionally
Because of all the wasted time that I had put into
Those cancelled projects
But she also hurt me emotionally
Because of how she continually said
Negative things about me that were unjustified
As she misjudged me which,
Ironically, is what my Mom used to do
Before her transformation.
It's been months since this happened
And now, dear Mom, because of the gift you
Have given to me, the gift of your acceptance and the
self-love that goes with it, I decided that I will finally
forgive this tortured woman for how she mistreated me
Because she couldn't help herself
Since she never got her mother to say to her
What she needed to hear.

Sadly, she will carry that disappointment in her heart
the rest of her life
Unless she gets unconditional love from a man
Or she finds a way to give it to others
Because by giving it to others
We give it to ourselves
Or if she gets help from a therapist who assists her in
working it out
Even though her mother is already gone
And she didn't get to hear the positive "Momisms" that
she needed to hear.

Yes, it's a lot harder to work these things out if you
failed to do it before someone has passed on
But she needs to do that or she will continue to reject
others the way she rejected me.

So, dear mother, I thank you for sharing your
encouraging Momisms while you were still alive.
I don't think it was just the dementia talking.
I think that was the you that you always
Wanted to be toward your devoted children,
The loving, positive you.

So, dear reader, if there is someone in your life
That you care about,
—your mother, your father, your mother-in-law, your
father-in-law, your grandmother, your grandfather,
your child, your husband, your wife, your friend, your
sister, your brother, your cousin, your aunt, your uncle,
your colleague, your client, your customer, your
neighbor—
And she or he is saying nice things to you,
And about you,

Take the time to write down those nice things
So you can reread those words,
Through thick and thin,
So you will always have those caring words,
Whatever happens in the future.

And you can then reread those words
And keep it to yourself
Or you can share those words with others
If that feels appropriate and the right thing to do
As you forever recall the emotions
As well as the complex person
Who spoke or wrote those supportive words.

January 25, 2013

SIS

It's fun the way we call each other "Sis."
You call me "Sis"
And I call you "Sis."

It's been so long since we've used each other's names
But of course you are and always will be
"My sister Eileen"
Like the famous play about the sisters
Living in Manhattan
As single career women.

We didn't get to do that
Since we both married so young
Although your marriage stuck
And my first one did not.

But we did live just a block away from each other
In lower Manhattan for a couple of years
And it was wonderful to be so close to
Each other again
Although not as close as the 16 years
We shared a room
In that little three bedroom house in Queens
Where we grew up
During our collective childhood.

What would our relationship have been like
If our older brother had lived past 23?
Would you and I have grown as close as we have
become since Seth's passing
Challenged to find commonalities despite our
completely opposite temperaments

For it was suddenly just the two of us
As we were determined to keep
Our sibling bond going and growing.

I'm glad we found a way to become close again
Even though I'm the artist and the dreamer
And you're the practical government employee
Working at the same agency for almost forty years.

There's a side of me that envies your stability
Although I know that's a path that I could not have
Taken and I admire the tact with which you handle people and situations
So often finding a way to work things out
And responding to comments with wit and
Presence of mind,
A sharp contrast to me who often thinks of what
I should have said,
but it may be hours or even a day or two after the fact.

We don't look alike
Although we used to both have brown hair.
Now yours is salt and pepper gray
And mine would be too
If I didn't choose to cover the gray.

We dress differently
And I watch a lot more TV than you do since
You still read the most books a week
Than anyone I know
Except for my husband who is also an avid reader.

We're like that song where
One person says "potato" and

The other pronounces it "potato"
with an emphasis on the "tot" sound
But our differences, I have grown to realize,
As together we shared the death of
Our brother, father and, just two weeks ago,
Of our mother,
Are very superficial.

On the deepest level,
We are cut from the same cloth
Since we have shared those earliest childhood
memories, experiences that will always bond us
Whether it's the camps we went to together
Or the summer home we both loved to visit
That unfortunately our Mom decided we
we would no longer retreat too way too soon.
And we've shared the birth of our children
And our marriages
And the extended family
That we share and include.

I don't know what it would be like to have been
An only child
I know friends and cousins would have been
Much more important to me
But I'm so glad I did not have to find out
Because I have an older sister
Just 17 months older than me
With whom I shared my childhood
And with whom I still share my adult years.

January 25, 2013

CHANCE MEETING

I was sitting at the restaurant at the Nashville Airport
Listening to the country musicians playing
Their guitars and singing
As I waited for my flight to Florida
Four hours later.

I purposely arrived early at the airport
Since I was tired of being alone in our apartment
Without any friends in the new building yet
With my husband already away on a business
trip in California
And I knew that people tend to be friendlier and chatty
at the airport.

At that inviting restaurant with the live music blaring I
ordered the appetizer platter,
A greasy array of fried foods —chicken fingers,
chicken wings, and fried onion rings —
Far different from my usual
Diet-conscious fair of salad and broiled
Chicken with balsamic vinegar on the side.

"This is comfort food,"
I boldly said to the attractive woman with blonde
hair sitting by herself next to me.
It was hard to hear our voices over the loud
music but we were both going to try.

"My mother died two weeks ago so I'm eating comfort
food," I continued.

"My father died ten years ago and it took me two years to get over it," she quickly volunteered.

"Is your mother still alive?" I asked.
"Yes," she replied.
"How old is she?"
"73."
"That's so young," I responded.
"My mother was 90," I quickly added.

She went on to tell me that it didn't
Really matter about her mother's age
Because she didn't have anything to do
With her mother.

"My mother left me with my father
When I was eight," she explained.
"I didn't see my mother again till I was 40."

I assured her that there was still time to try to build
A relationship with her mother,
Since her mother was only 73,
before it was too late.

She disagreed.
She answered, adamantly,
"I needed my mother when I was eight,
I needed my mother when I was 10,
I needed my mother when I was 15,
I don't need my mother now."

She shared with me that she was very successful —CEO of a surgery center

In a wealthy town in California
And before that she was head of
A hospital.
She didn't mention anything about her family life to
me and I felt uncomfortable asking her if she was
married or if she had children,
but I was curious to know if that was true.

I gave her my "pitch" about the benefits of working
things out with your mother,
while you still have the chance,
even if her Mother made mistakes,
sharing about how these unresolved family
relationships can impact on other relationships
and even on our work or careers and even our health
in the most unsuspecting ways.

But this stranger did not want to hear my message,
she was not ready to hear my suggestion,
she was still too angry at her mother,
still too unforgiving.

Dressed in all black, she gathered up her coat
and her black suitcase
and she wished me well as she left
to catch her plane home.

After she left, I looked over at her table
Where she had also been eating comfort food—
A huge basket of french fries and a plate
of fried appetizers including chicken fingers—
already removed from her table
But her pink drink was still there,

Just about a third of it left in the distinctive-looking glass,
A glass with a wide bottom and a long
Narrow neck to the stem.

I asked the waitress what the drink was called
And she told me it was called a "Cosmo,"
So I looked it up in the menu.

I found out that the drink was made with vodka and cranberry juice,
And I wondered, to myself,
What psychic pain she needed to be in to have to subdue it by drinking vodka all by herself
at the airport on a weekday at just 3 o'clock in the afternoon.

I could only hope that maybe she would give her
Mother another chance
As someday she might remember what we had talked about,
Someday when she might finally be ready to try to work things out with her mother so she
Could find the peace I had told her that I had found
Because I worked things out with my mother
The peace that only happens if you've
Found a way to work out the bulk of your parent-child issues while both of you are still alive.
.

January 26, 2013

GRIEF

Intellectually I was ready to get back to work after a few days of mourning.
I told myself that *shiva* was a wise concept
Because it meant that when I stopped sitting *shiva*
I would be ready to rejoin the world.

But that's not what my mind and body told me.
It's been a few weeks and I'm still in a bathrobe.
My concentration is very poor,
And I've watched more mindless TV in a few weeks
Than in a few years.

But I know, just today, I'm turning the corner
On this grief thing:
I washed the sink full of dishes.
No one had to tell me to do that,
I just did it
Because suddenly the dirty dishes were annoying me.

I feel like a big baby who misses her mother.
I want my mother to hug me,
To tell me I'm wonderful,
And to ask me, "How was your day at school?"
Or "What's new with the kids?"
But she won't ever be able to ask me those
Questions again.

I know it hit me hard when my brother died,
But it was such a dramatic death
That little was said about it.
I just kept going
All those many years ago

When I was twenty
And my older brother died at twenty three.

Then, when my father died,
My children were still young,
Just six and ten,
So I had to get it together,
To keep the household going,
To be a wife,
And a mother,
And that was what stopped me from
Staying in bed for days on end.

But now that the kids are grown
And no one needs me anymore
I can give in to my grief
My shock
My sadness
That my sister and I are orphans now.
Both are parents are gone.
Father's Day and Mother's Day
Will always have a different meaning for us now.

I realize I'm staying in bed
And sleeping
And grieving
For all those times that I had to push those sad
Feelings deep inside
And keep going
When I really just wanted to pull away from the world
And feel sorry for myself
And my loss.

When is it time to say "enough?"

"Grief, let go of me? I want to go forward?"
Is it after a month? Two months?
Six months? A year?

It's up to each of us to know when we are ready to move on
But I know this time I want to allow myself to thoroughly mourn
My mother's death four weeks ago
At the age of ninety.
Yes, a ripe old age, so many have said to me,
But, to me, it was still too soon to say goodbye.
So, this time, I want to do my "grief work" now
Instead of avoiding those feelings
Only to have the unresolved grief turn into
A physical or psychic pain
That never seems to go away.

I've learned these last four weeks that
I can cry without tears.

February 11, 2013

A GRANDPARENT'S LOVE

What an honor to be in his life from the very beginning
To watch him grow
Transforming from a newborn to
Learning to walk
To talking
To developing a personality all his own
And an amazing vocabulary
And even being able to write
Words and draw pictures
All by the age of three.

As busy I might be with work
Or other relationships
I will always find a way to make time
To visit my grandson.

Thank you, son, for asking me to
Be such a big part of your lives.

I'm glad I allow myself
To share by phone
And in visits
Even if for now it has to be long distance.

I will visit as often as time and money permit
Because I love my grandson and my son
very much and being around my grandson makes me
feel young again.

January 27, 2013

RETURNING TO MY WORK AS AN ARTIST

I just discovered dozens and dozens of drawings rolled up in several piles
I must have thrown those oversized pages into the boxes that I took from my mother's attic.

I haven't looked at those drawings for decades
Since I first drew those images during my art classes at college
Or the life drawing sessions I used to go to.

Now I am looking at these black-and-white charcoal life studies
And the pencil drawings of still lives
And I see those models that I sketched
As if it was yesterday
Instead of 40 years ago.

Time is frozen in those drawings
Time and a talent that I set aside
To pursue the written word
Instead of visual images.

I made my choice
I just couldn't answer to two such demanding masters
And still have a life
But I have raised my children
And my husband is busy with his job
So I can once again allow myself to get drawn into
That demanding and all-consuming obsession
Of drawing, sketching, painting,
And creating collages.

I pick up a tube of acrylic paint—
I even remember when I bought it,
It was to paint the last major painting that I created
More than 20 years ago—
And the paint is still soft
As if I bought the tube yesterday.
It is like a new tube,
"Light portrait pink"
A color the lets me paint flesh tones without
Having to mix the paint.

I now long to return to creating art
But I know it will take time to rekindle those visual
and physical muscles.
The power of concentration that I once had,
The visual intensity,
The fingers and hands once so limber and driven to
draw that I filled up a sketch book every week or so
As I now recall those days when I carried around
A sketchpad so I would create a sketch
Whenever the spirit moved me
Just like I now write down words and thoughts
In my written journals or in my iPhone.
I am starting to remember that other "me"
That was the art student.
The recluse,
The self-contained lonely soul
Who could spend two days completely
Absorbed in finishing a painting,
Not saying a word to anyone
Including the graduate student and boyfriend
With whom I was living at the time.

The writer me is a much more outgoing creator
Even though writing can be solitary
But it is the nature of writing that I am forced to
interact more than I had to as an artist.

Is that why I pulled away from the visual
And the cerebral and gravitated instead to words?

For now, I will start to fill in the oversized unfinished
pencil drawing of a leaf
that I started so many years before
As I smile with pride that I am the artist who created
That drawing oh so many years ago.

I find a green pencil and fill in two leaves
And then one stem but I stop myself.
I don't feel that same compulsion that I used to feel
and I don't want to force my creativity.

Still, I'm so glad I kept these rolled up sketches
Even if it took six years since I brought those drawings
home to look at each roll.
I just need to be ready to let that other "me" back in.

February 12, 2013

THE VICTIM

It is the most famous case of its kind in years:
An Olympic superstar shoots and kills his girlfriend.
Was it an accident?
Was it intentional?
The judge will ultimately decide
But whatever happens to the shooter
This lovely, caring, beautiful young woman is dead.

Her life was cut short
By bullets and confusion.
If those bullets had just hit her in her leg
Or her arm or missed her all together
It would be such a different story
A sad story but one with at least the chance of a happy ending.

There can be no happy ending for Reeva, the victim,
For her parents, her brother, her friends, her colleagues
for Reeva is no more
And I will forever feel sad about that.
A woman I have never met,
A woman I have never known,
Because she is yet another innocent victim
Whether it was an accident or intentional
The end result is the same: a full and promising life cut short.

RIP Reeva.
You will be missed
You will be mourned
But you will not be forgotten.

February 22, 2013

WHY I WRITE

"Why do I write?" a sixth grader asked me.
Initially, I was speechless.
Then I replied,
"What an interesting question?"
As I asked, rhetorically, "Why do I write?"

I write because not writing
is harder for me than writing.

I write to inspire.

I write to express myself,
my feelings,
my joy,
my pain,
my anger,
my bliss.

I write because so many writers have given so much to
me through their writing.

I write to share.

I write to distill my experiences
and record my impressions.

Writing is challenging,
demanding,
hard,
competitive,
exacting work,
but how many can say

they can't wait to start their job each day?

How many can say they are totally engrossed
in what they do,
Rather than watching the clock for quitting time?

How many can say that they are proud of what
they accomplish by their work?

As a writer, I can say all those things are true,
and more.

Writers are, of course, not the only ones
who feel pride and joy in their work.

There are glorious occupations and avocations
galore,
from teachers and nurses, doctors, and therapists to
TV commentators, plumbers, carpenters,
or explorers.

For me, writing is the way I express myself best
And the way I feel I am making a difference in the
world,
Trying to make it a better place.
The writing I do now is probably the most
Glorious writing I have ever done
Because my life is so joyful
That I write out of happiness and the love of words
And not out of loneliness or pain.

I write because it enables me to be in two places at
once
I'm doing whatever I'm doing right now

But my writing,
All my various writing, is working for me,
In all parts of the world in many foreign languages.

I write because of the doors it opens.
I write because of the people I get to meet and
the places I get to visit,
In reality, or in my imagination.

I write as a way of saying, "Jan Yager is here."

I write because crafting a sentence
And rewriting words until I get the right one
Can be as fulfilling as making sure I use the right
paint for a painting
Or the right tool for a sculpture.

I write because it enables me to control the words that I commit to
To get it right and fine tune the nuances
of what I intended to say.

I write because I can't not write.

April 26, 2001
(Written in response to my guest talk on writing at
Mr. C's classes on April 25th)

FOR THE LOVE OF A CAT

I used to think I wasn't a "cat person."
I grew up surrounded by dogs.
First there was Lassie.
I don't remember her
But I've heard my Mother
Talk about her over the years.

Then there was Queenie.
I loved that dog
But she was run over by a bread delivery man.

Then there was Wags.
I called her Wag Tail Lee Barkas I.
I dressed her up for Halloween and taught
her how to twirl.

I loved my little dog Love
And then there was Plato.

My friend Paula got scratched by a cat when we were
Little and because of that,
I always feared cats.

So imagine my surprise when I fell in love with
The love of my life
And he had two cats,
Jeremiah Johnson and Brigitte for Brigitte Bardot.

So here I was,
Face to face with a dilemma.
And I chose the new experience, deciding
That my wonderful new mate Fred

had to know something I did not yet know
or he wouldn't have been a "cat person."

It didn't take long before I myself saw the wonder of
cats: independent yet loving,
Self-sufficient yet loyal.
Quieter and more subtle than dogs,
Yet devoted companions.

Fred's cats also taught me about coping with death
For when they both died, it was wrenching and sad.
In a short period of time, I had gotten completely
devoted to each cat.
But their illnesses because of old age were so
debilitating and
Death came without warning for the first one
And faster for the second but
It was inevitable in the scheme of things.

Years later, our sons' babysitter, Val, asked permission
To let the boys have kittens as a gift
And we said "yes."
And I discovered the distinctive personalities of first
L.J. and then Kimberly
And when L.J. died of cancer just nine years later,
It was so very very painful.

Kimberly clings to us more after her soulmate LJ is gone.
I talk to Kimberly, I pet her,
And I give her treats every now and then.

I wonder why or how I could have spent so many years
Unaware of the wonders of cats.
I'm glad since the age of thirty-five
I see why cats are so splendid.

They say there are "cat people" and "dog people"
But I see that even if the pets may have different traits and needs
They all share one thing with their owners: a wish to love and be loved,
To be cherished and attended to.

It's a mutual admiration society, without words,
with nonverbal communication of the highest order.

Since we can give and receive so much love from our pets without words
We need to remember that with our human loved ones
as we prompt ourselves to go beyond words
and show our love more often
through our actions.

July 15, 2004

FRIENDSHIFTS

I am reminded of what my girlfriend Ginny said when
My husband and best friend Fred and I drove
Down from Connecticut in rush hour traffic on a weekday night
To attend her father's wake at a funeral home in Queens
When Ginny took my hand, looked me square in the eye,
and said, "You don't need a lot of friends. Just a few good ones."

And I was happy I made that long trip,
And I was proud I was there for Ginny when she needed me
And it was okay that we don't see each other all the time the way we did when we were
Children spending almost every day after school together
During our elementary school years
Because Ginny knew my late brother,
And Ginny knew my first husband,
And I knew her parents and her brother and her sister,
And I was at Ginny's wedding,
And she and her husband were there for mine, and we get together with Fred, my second husband.

And Ginny was there for my sons' bar mitzvah,
And my mother's 85th birthday party,
And, five years later, my mother's funeral,
'Cause Ginny knew me when we were next door neighbors and childhood best friends and blood sisters

When it was still okay to prick your finger
And put our fingers together
And declare ourselves blood sister.

All those years ago when together with my sister
Eileen we watched *Mighty Joe Young* and *King Kong*
Twenty or thirty times on the *Million Dollar Movie*
On Channel 9 in Ginny's dark, cold basement in her
house that felt emotionally so warm
In that room that was our playroom for us all those
years.

Yes, friendshifts happen,
And that's okay
As long as we're there for each other,
On the phone
Or in person
Or over the Internet
So our friendship is still solid,
Even if it's changed.

911

I scan the paid obituaries in *The New York Times* today.
It is the biggest spread I've ever seen.
Column after column of entries.
A few died of "natural causes" at age 80, 90, and even 95,
But most are men, and some women, in their prime,
30, 40, 50 years old,
And they all have the same date of death,
September 11th
A day that will live in infamy
Like December 7th, Pearl Harbor,
Or D-Day, or the day President Kennedy was shot.

Our nation, and the world, is changed forever.
What began as just another Tuesday at work
Or at school, turned into mayhem.

I have cried more in the last week than at any time since my father's death
Five years ago
But Dad died at 80, of cancer, not the victim of a terrorist bombing.

I am a visual person and I see so many men and women,
On the television,
In the special issues of *Time* and other magazines,
And in my imagination and day dreams,
Vibrant and caring,
Some resigned to their fate,
Most fighting the inevitable right till the end.

And I am haunted by those images.

Whether they died on the hijacked planes that crashed
Or in the fire or collapsed buildings that followed
There are no words
No explanations
No feelings
That express the despair I and so many are feeling.

And I was one of the lucky ones.
My husband, although nearby, on his way to the office building where he worked,
Down the street, when the planes crashed into the Twin Towers,
He managed to get out of harm's way
And to make his way uptown and
After an agonizing hour of silence and worry,
I got that phone call,
That phone call that so many were waiting for,
And I heard his voice,
And he said he was okay,
And that's all that mattered.

And my best friend from high school
Was not in the building when it happened
So she was okay
And so are her co-workers
But their office was destroyed.
But desks, files, and papers can be replaced,
But not the people.

When I was twenty, more than three decades ago,
My older brother was killed
And I felt afraid and scared

for many years but in time I regained my belief in a
"just world" and I was not scared anymore.

I want back the security I had found for myself
Before the September 11th attacks happened.
I want to feel carefree and unafraid again.
I long for the way New York City and Washington,
D.C. used to be.
Where are the missing people?
Where did they go?

When Fred's friend Charlie, an older man in his 70s
who used to be a coworker,
Died a few years ago,
He asked that his cremated ashes be
Spread at the race track around the statue of his
favorite race horse.
He wanted his ashes scattered around that beloved
statue that represented a place Charlie liked to go to
When he wasn't doing what he loved most, besides his
wife, being a reporter.

Now there are hundreds, thousands whose ashes
Are now part of that land, that city that
They all loved to work in,
Two buildings that used to be among
Just a handful of the most majestic and renowned
buildings in the world.

Everyone who personally lost a loved one, a spouse,
A child, a parent, a sibling, a friend,
A beloved co-worker who was more like a sister or a
brother,
A neighbor who was part of that community,

Will have to begin life anew, without that person, in their everyday activities,
And that is the ultimate loss.

But the world has dramatically changed for the rest of us as well.

I liked it better the way it was before.

September 18, 2001

THE SINGLE HOURS*

I glide through the morning
Tasting the sidewalks
And sniffing clutched newsprint.
Till mid afternoon
The hours gallop by.

But suddenly it is five
And workers seek their
Nocturnal retreats.
And now, for me,
Are the single hours.

Dinner alone.
I have nothing to say
To stainless steel
Or hastily prepared meals.
I sleep instead,
And awake
When others retire.

By ten I am rejuvenated.
Till morning, the hours are mine.
Read? Compose? Dance?
Dream? Paint? Socialize?

Finally an old friend calls.
"Join me for coffee?"
No, I prefer solitude.
I need to be touched,
Not heard.

The single hours return.

*Published in *Today's Single* newspaper.

One to eight. Silent pavement,
The cravings filled by wrapped promises
The clock seems to move in
Syncopated half time.
I think of that man in Italy
I once read about who had not
Slept in twelve years,
And I know it might be worse.

I long to shake hands with
My time alone for only then
Will I want, not need, to be
With someone else.

DEADLINES

My first published works were in
Elementary school in *The Scribe*.
Poems and short stories and essays.
I also kept a journal and
wrote to "Di"
my thoughts and hopes and anxieties.

Then one day I was published
For the world to read,
Published in journals and books
And magazines.

Now I write assignments.
Most are my own ideas
But I've gotten further and
Further from the catharsis
That writing used to be.

Writing was different when the
Act itself sustained me.
Writing had a quiet, perfect
Quality to it as I felt broadened
And valued by committing my thoughts
To the page.

Of course now I rewrite, and rewrite,
To say my thought in the best possible way
 But the thoughts do not change, only the delivery.

However somehow in redoing all those single thoughts
I feel I've lost other thoughts in-between.
No one asks me about art or poetry any more,

It's economics and finance, and how to get a job.
But I still think of those questions
I had hoped to provoke through my work,
like love, and honor, and the uniqueness
of those we love.

Writing for a living,
And writing to be published,
It's writing,
But it's not the same as when
I wrote for just "Di,"
"Di," the all listening, nonjudgmental diary.

SELF-LOVE

I dream of loving myself
The way I wish he would,
The way my Mother never could.

I fantasize about being strong
And finding it is in my own heart
That I belong.

I think of the me that
We know is there.
The me that makes him care.

That me is beautiful and
Loving and fair.
That me does not despair.

Sometimes I feel a surge of love
And I do not ask, "Am I right?"
That woman is secure.

It happens more frequently now
Than it ever has before
But I know it should be more.

I want to be whole
And strong and free
To give, and get, love from me.

IN QUARANTINE

Writers are a strange breed.
We isolate ourselves
To describe people.

Why does segregation
At the keyboard
Unwittingly threaten virility?
Will printed pages compensate
For caressing arms,
Infant gurgles,
And growing rebellion?

I find one kind of immortality.
But is life after life
Enough to keep me going?
Must rewrites negate reverence?
Will bylines bypass babes?

I do not wish worldly worship
I compose to share—
Visions, pathos, and notions.
Yet my mailbox is filled more
Than any other part of me.

Have we found each other?
Will you see that I pulsate
After the typewriter is silent?

A DISAGREEMENT WITH HOMANS' EXCHANGE THEORY OF SATIATION

Homan's theory used to make sense to me:
That one unit of anything is, relatively,
Far more than three.

But since I met Him
I must disagree—
The twentieth time he says "I love you"
Is far *more* valuable to me.

For each unit is not, in truth,
The same.
Qualitatively the words
Differ and deepen
As do my feelings when I hear his name.

Homans may have been right
About material things
But not about feelings
Or romantic activities.

MISSING YOU

Is it just a week since last we spoke?
It seems so much longer.
I miss you, dearest, with all my heart,
My need to talk with you grows stronger.

I wish I knew where to call
But alas that is not wise.
Yet I want so much to hear your voice,
Your words, your thoughts, your cries.

Sweet gentle man, your touch is strong
And your heart bigger still.
I fear for you, for me, for us.
Don't let time and others our friendship kill.

Your soul is so dear to me
It has penetrated my deepest core.
Your letters are so passionate
I want more and more and more.

What will we feel or do, my dear,
Just a year from now?
Will we be friends, lovers, mates,
Or thoughts of "I wonder how...?"

Inside my heart and guts I feel this need
To reach out and speak with you.
It's fired up by my sincere belief
That you feel this way too.

It is so rare, as well we know,
that two souls feel the same.

Whatever happens, kind caring man,
It's you, and your life, that I do wish to
Join together within a frame.

So forgive me, friend, for needing you
And wanting you so.
I miss you, my love,
Whether right or wrong
That is the truth I want you to know.

I miss you, my friend,
With a love and need
That I know I should not dare.
Forget me, if you must,
I will understand,
For I feel loved and excited forever
Because of the grasp of your hand.

It's only been a day since your last letter
And yet I miss your new thoughts so.
I crave your words and elegant script
As perhaps only you could know.

I will try not to abandon you
Whatever sacrifices that will mean.
What anguish or wonders will occur because of that
Remains to be seen.

ODE TO LOVE

I hope you'll always want to meet my train
For I will never forget what it was like
Before you were in my life.

We're both romantics
But you may have met your match.

Nurture me
I'll nurture you
As we nurture ourselves,
With the familiar and the new.

NEW ROMANCE

No one can force it.
It knows no reason.
You said we could have been right
But not this season.

I am receptive,
You are afraid.
I am courageous,
You are staid.

The intertwining of our souls
Is exhilarating to me.
To you, I fear, it is
A grave responsibility.

You said we are not children
So we should already be sure.
I say new love takes time
Whether fifteen or sixty-four.

So let's have fun
And not hold back.
Banish her face and form
It is faith in love you lack.

Give in, my sweet,
And see what realities are in store.
Perhaps those feelings will be better
Than the fantasies of before.

You say you are not in love with me
No doubt you think that true.

I say, trust that there are many kinds of love,
Quite foreign to what we both knew.

Please do not tell me what or who I need,
And I will also let you be.
Risk and dare,
Love and care,
You can not control or protect me.

LOVE SLIPPED AWAY

Love slipped away
The other day
More gently than it came.
But in my heart
I felt him part
His touch, his lips were not the same.

I've thought about those hours together.
I've searched for some clear reason.
Alas, there is no definite one,
It was just not our season.

Our time for making love
And loving and caring and
Cooing and sharing
Had gone.
It went away, 'tis sad, I know,
But 'tis sadder to hold on.

I wonder if he knows it yet
For I saw it in his eyes.
It pains me to think of him suffering so,
But I cannot help him
For it is me that he has to forget.

Perhaps he will not close his heart
As he closed his lips last time.
Perhaps he will face his fears
And let love grow with time.

His gentleness he showed to me
And that so many men find frightening.

My head is spinning as I tearfully say the words,
"Love slipped away,"
Slipped away like lightening.

Why did it flee, my dearest one?
Why did you hide from our life together?
I would have done most anything
If you had only not run.

Maybe you thought it would all go away,
Or mend on its own.
Maybe you thought
Just calling and caring
Would nurture us alone.

But, love, you have to grow
With me as I must grow with you.
And growth needs open doors
Not dark hallways
If we are to come through anew.

Just as I caught glimpses of your heart
You closed it off to me.
With labels that falsely classify
The me you fear to see.

My love you came so close to me
But not quite close enough.
1 thought, for once, I had found a deep love
And this time it was not a bluff.

Silently I will wait for you
To catch up to my feelings.
But I cannot wait too much longer

Because I need love too.

So take a week, two weeks, or more
And look into your heart.
Find the answers within yourself
That tell you that you never want to be apart.

I know that now but I know it just for me
And just for one is not enough.
Realize the joyfulness that we can have
Before our world becomes a dot.

You have been and still are my world
And yet we both know
It is quickly shrinking.
Gain hold and embrace our love
And give up that time just thinking.

I knew it when your lips failed to open
And take my soul in yours.
But I flew from that pain
Hoping it would not return again
But tonight I became certain.

Why did you change
And turn around
When all seemed to be going for the best?
Why are you closing
The open book that
Speaks of all the rest?

My love, you are a fool sometimes
And this is one of those plays.
You ask to be alone

When these should be our together days.

I cry thinking of the months we've spent
Coming toward to only go even further away.
Tell me if that is what you wish and
We will start afresh,
Separate, and searching
For that other one with whom
You and I were meant.

NATURE'S LISP

The clouds know,
The birds tell.
The sea beckons,
The winds blow.

The trees dream,
The leaves flutter.
The night haunts,
The insects scream.

The hills climb,
The valleys rest.
The rain laughs,
The snowflakes rhyme.

The flower cries,
The seeds sow,
The passion ends,
The love dies.

WINTER

Like the overture to an operetta,
The first snowflakes stroke the sloping window.
Joyous eyes watch the swirling crystals
Become embryonic droplets prancing
Along the roof.

Waiting breasts press the glass,
Studying the graceful dancers that
Massage half naked trees,
Tickling frozen months ahead
Till another act begins.

At last the longing for love replaces arousal
As I await his return.
But we did not share this first celestial fondling.

The woods are now gray.
Leaves occasionally toss
Like a child's flippers through water.
Deep etchings become a smile
As his tires dig into firm ground
Bringing his gentle hands
Closer, sooner, nearer, dearer.

THE HARDEST KIND OF LOVE

The easiest kind of love
Is the love that's not returned.
Oh there's pain and sadness
And yearning and wishing
But it's always self-contained.

There's no risk in one-way love,
You know what's going to be.
You can be certain of the outcome
—No outcome, that is—
For the loved one can not
Set forth his life and
Let his feelings run free.

I've known so many who spend their lives
Mistaken in thinking that
They did love
Because they knew one, or more,
Of the one-way kind.

But the hardest love is not unrequited,
It is returned and shared.
For then the lovers know its preciousness
And at first one or both may be scared.

Scared of giving,
And scared of taking.
Scaring of speaking,
And scared of faking.
Scared of longing,
And scared of needing,
Scared of sharing,

And scared of deceiving.
Scared of having,
And scared of losing.
Scared of finding,
And scared of misusing.
Scared of hurting,
And scared of flirting.
Scared of flaunting,
And scared of misconstruing.
Scared of competing,
And scared of misleading.
Scared of pushing,
And scared of punishing.
Scared of feeling,
And scared of misreading.

Yet I have just discovered
That to be scared is not so bad
For being scared at least shows life,
And life shows hope
And the chance not to be sad.

He hurt me and I hurt back
But soon we came together anew.
And so it proved indeed the
Hardest kind of love.
So we both care and love
In a way that is bewildering and
Glorious and totally new.

When I came home on Friday
And saw him sitting there,
Flowers in his hand,
I knew that I was right to

Face the lions and
Find out just how far
This feeling will land.

It was a wondrous weekend
And for once I looked at
The plus
I put the minuses away
And found a new calculator today.

This one racks up the beauteous times,
The positive and the fulfilling.
It sets aside the pettiness
And says "Yes, I'm willing."

Willing to open up my heart
And this time go the distance.
But go the distance may not prove
To be the one I set
For this time love is a two-way
Pact and his distance
Is one I have not yet met.

His distance includes
A collection of others—
Sisters, parents, friends,
And brothers.
A world outside the bedroom walls,
A man that breathes, triumphs,
And even falls.

I've yet to see him fall,
That much trust he does
Not give me yet,

But when he does I will
Find out if I can give to him
When his deepest self calls.

I've shown him weakness,
And maybe he will realize
As I have,
That in stressing the former
I have not shown him me.

For sometimes it is harder
To give cheer instead of solace
For we may panic at the
Autonomy of others
Just as the mother mourns
And rejoices as the
Toddler takes on the
World alone.

I tell you of a wondrous man,
 A sweet and caring soul.
A tortured man,
A joyful man,
A man whose heart I behold.

He offers me a chance to grow
For so much have I thus far changed.
I wonder if he realizes
Through my growth we both
Will gain.

I deeply hurt him recently
And in so doing
His pain hurt me.

It was then I knew
Deep down in my core
What I had always been
Told, "You're not the same,
If you love, as you were before."

I look different to myself,
At peace and at war,
I see the change
But doubt that others
Can see into that core.

But he can see
And I allow him
And that frightens both
Of us more than
What he'll find.

Sometimes I want to squeeze him
Because I find it overpowering,
This feeling that I've just discovered,
This hardest kind of love.

The facility I have with words
Are both a blessing and a curse
For I can toss off thoughts to him,
And have to wait until he finds
His own way to toss them
Back my way again.

He found a way,
A simple bouquet,
Those fourteen stems
Said more than fourteen

Stanzas, or three hundred more.

I wish he could just for a moment share
The rapture in my heart
When I saw those flowers
And saw the pubescent
Excitement that he
Brought to them and to me.

The words flow
Because the feelings surge up
And out and since he left
They have no where to go.
But yet they go into this page
And somehow that emotion
Will reach him again.

If I do not send this poem to
Him it matter not,
For the hardest kind of
Love, and yet the simplest
Kind, cannot be bought
For a word or a song.
It has to grow and
Growth takes time.
It grows unwittingly,
Or it grows when it
Is ready to climb.

He may not be ready yet
And whether that day will
Ever come,
I know it will,
But cannot swear to that

And yet this hardest kind of
Love suggests
It may not extinguish no matter
What he or I do.

For with each step,
And with each stage,
We grow together,
And toward the grave.
I think of death
Not because I am maudlin,
But because I see us together,
They're to rest.

A lifetime with him
Would not be too long,
For those fourteen stems
Came from a man whose
Soul is endless.

I see that soul
And I know that's why he's scared,
For I love the him
That no one else has known
Is there.

And I know his secrets
Even though they've never been said,
For I see into that soul,
And I hear him without words.

For decades he, as I,
Have known only the simplest kind of love
And so we have no preparation f or

What we are going through.
Since he is why
I feel this way,
And I am the cause for him,
In this vital matter
Unlike all else,
I cannot turn to him.

He has become my very best friend,
A phrase I do not lightly use,
And yet when it comes to loving him,
I, like he, am alone.

But this time I am alone with my love
Not because it is a fantasy.
I am alone with my love
because for me, and for him,
it opens up the galaxy.

It took thousands of years to
Evolve the earth
And sadly that much time I
Will not have.
But a year or two or three or more
Is not too long to create
My new universe.
A universe filled with Us
But one that
Never denies the I.
That is a quest
Few do achieve
For most find longing
And wanting too traumatic
To let love succeed.

They settle for the simplest love
And live with regrets or dreams.
They give up the pain
But they also lose the ecstasy
And so they lose it all.

I cannot mock those who
Chose that path
For I used to walk by their side.
It was safer then,
But I was oh so alone,
And oh so very much a half.

Today the "two halves
Becoming one" is
Unpopular and demeaned
As individuals say
"I have me, that's all
I need."
But having "Me" means
Being with another
And so that me can
Only be a cover.
A cover for something
Not quite right,
A cover to hold back
The uncertainty of love.

I look at the unknown future
And I laugh at my former fears
For only by walking through
Those shadows
Will his image reappear.
Reappear to stay the night

Stay the week
Stay the life.
Reappear to share the wows,
Reappear to cushion the blows.
Reappear to make me soup,
Reappear to want my joy.
Reappear to scratch my head,
Reappear to hear my sighs,
Reappear to share my bed.

Reappear to clear the dishes
Reappear to appease my wishes.
Reappear to mirror my pleas,
Reappear to bring me to my knees.
Reappear to increase the joy,
Reappear to bring me a toy.

But if this hardest love of all
Proves false or only one-sided,
I will put away this poem
And look for someone with whom
"My wife" he will call.

For I am ready as I have never been
To get on with living as it
Always might have been.
But "might have been" is the saddest of
Phrases and I no longer have to
Look back or forward,
Mourning those unseen, or unfound, paths.

So, sweet, loving man,
Take your time
For hard-found love

Cannot be quickly lost.
I trust your mind,
And I trust your heart,
And I trust what
Thus far I've been told.

I know a bit of what
You are going through
For in some way I am
Going through it too.
But the wonder and the
Bane of loving as we do
Is that close as we are—
And as we will someday be—
I am Im and you are still
You, and four or five, not
One, can we be.

I'm not running away again,
I won't do that to us,
For never would I—or you know—
if I—or you—
Decided to refrain.

You say you are a "little" trapped
As if you feel that alone.
Would I still be completely
A solo if I had needed—
Or wanted—a someone
In my home?

You'll find, sweet man,
In this hardest love
That feelings—great or

sour—are more often
Than not shared.
For what makes it all the harder
Is that I, like you, seem to
Always be there.

Be there in my thoughts,
Be there in my sighs,
Be there in my fears,
Be there in my cries,
Be there in my tomorrows,
Be there in my dreams,
Be there in my every move
Be there in my tears.

I write these thoughts to this paper
What I could not—dare not—say
To your flesh
For loving is, I've found,
Also holding back
And this pouring forth would
Bewilder you even more.

You know I am unique and terrific,
You know I am your love.
It is that that frightens you
And causes you to hide?

I cannot say, "Hide no more
And all will be so splendid."
For two, not one, is not
Yet what you have intended.

I stand aside as much as you heed

Wanting to help
But knowing there is nothing
I can do but watch you bleed.

Watch and wait and
Tell myself
That someday I'll be there.
Hoping—believing—that
It comes true
Because you finally dare:
Dare to love,
And dare to hurt,
Dare to share,
And dare to feel.
Dare to care,
And dare to want,
Dare to wish,
And dare to scream.

I want to hear your screams,
My love,
And not just all your jokes.
You need someone who can
See that part of you
And help you laugh at it too.

So I wait—and work—and
Love you from afar
But when we are together
I feel your love for me.
And that is what makes it
So very hard
For I, you see,
Am just as scared as you.

Yet I had the courage to
Tip the scales
For love is like
A justice weight
If one side is heavier than
The other,
That lighter side must weight.

So I tipped the scales,
So you could rise,
Soaring as you want and can.
I'm lighter now
So you can grow heavy
If that is how you feel.

We'll see, my dear,
And no matter what
The answer will never be phony
For you—as I love you so much—
That alone we intimately share.

For now I know what
People mean
When they say love is sharing.

They don't mean sharing "experiences"
Or jobs or vacations or friends
Or sports or books.
They mean sharing the caring,
The loving, and the pain.
Sharing the feelings that
Come but once if they come at all.

That kind of sharing cannot die.
It thrives, and grows, on its own.
So, in trust, my dear,
I end this poem,
Written for you, and me,
As I reread these words alone.

THE BIRD FEEDER

A blue grey gnatcatcher
Rests upon its man-made house,
Assures his safety and
Snatches seeds and grains.

Stay away or
Your food will be stolen.

I too fear someone
Will take my sustenance
Just as I have some safety.

But he returns
Again.

Oh how long it has been
Between feedings.

IF ONLY HE WANTED TO BE WITH ME

If only he wanted to be with me
I'd say to him, with a twinkle in my voice,
"How did your day go, dear?"
We'd chat,
We'd kiss,
We'd squeeze each other
And we'd be glad that now,
After the day of others had ended,
We had our together time.

If only he wanted to be with me,
I'd fill his minutes with restful sighs,
I'd fill his glass with soothing liquids,
I'd fill his mouth with satisfying kisses.

But alas he prefers to be alone
Or with a friend or two or three.
"Be patient," he says,
"You demand too much."
I do, I know.
I demand what I want to give:
Evenings and weekends of together alone time.
It would make the time out there
So much more pleasant
For it would not be all there is.

Today I faced the sad painful truth
That he does not need, or want, me
As much as I want him.

I do not fault my love for that
For someday he will have that crying urge,

That need, that wanting that demands being together.

Sometimes I wonder how we two
So close in so many thoughts and feelings
Could be so separate on how much time
We want to spend together.

My girlfriend tells me of a man
She is not that attracted to.
He wants to spend all his time with her
And she, like my lover, longs for her alone time
And for someone she really wants.

It pains me to think that he
Might be thinking the same thing about me.

THE IDEA THIEF

As skillful as the most proficient cat burglar
The idea thief gains your trust
So you share your ideas without fear
Only to find he or she takes credits for what
You contributed.

You will find the idea thief in the workplace
Or reaching out to you on the Internet
Or bending your ear at a networking event.
So be careful about what you share
Especially in your brags
Because you never know what idea thief
Is lurking around the corner.

How do you know if someone's an idea thief?
You can try to trick this predator by sharing
An insignificant idea and see if he or she
Shares it without giving you credit.
Then you will know not to be as open
And trusting with your original ideas
That you have labored so long and hard to develop
That you do not want the idea thief passing along
As his or her own.

February 27, 2013

CHILDREN'S DAY

On Mother's Day children thank their mothers
And that's what the tradition many think should be,
But I see it differently
And want to thank my children
For letting me become a mother
so I get to be part of another world
That being a parent let's me see.

Instead of being stuck in just one generation
I get to share the joys and challenges that they face.
Being a mother has given me so much joy and love
And pride in my two sons
As I applaud them for being their unique selves
And rejoice that at least for our family
We try not to make it too competitive a race.

Through fun times and tough times,
Through trips and family dinners,
Being a mother is always a magical experience for me
Because by becoming parents
My husband and I are definitely
The winners.

When I've proposed the idea of Children's Day
To other mothers or fathers they gasp and disagree.
"Every day is children's day" they say,
"I want a day that just celebrates me."

I try to explain that without a child
Mother's Day has a different meaning.

They understand that
but they want gifts and cards and eating out
And credit for all they did and do
Including going through weaning.

I'm not a martyr and that's not why I say
There should be a Children's Day.
It's just that so many parents put a guilt trip on their
children when they repeat again and again
"Look at all I've done for you."

I'm just saying let's make it fair
And look at what we do for each other—
Children add so much to a mother's life
Whether you have one child or five.
Each one is so special and amazing
He or she could not be replaced by another.

Yes, it's a mutual admiration society
This thing called parenting:
Parents are fortunate to have their children and
children are blessed to have their mothers and fathers.
So I humbly request that we have
A day that we call "Children's Day"
Just like we have Mother's Day and Father's Day
And even Grandparents day
So we parents can send cards and say all the
Cute and sentimental thoughts
About how much we appreciate our children
That we should all be saying every day.

Happy Children's Day to my children and my
grandson and to all the children of the world.

February 27, 2013

GROWING UP*

How lavish this room used to be.
My kingdom flourished within these walls.
The doorknobs opened up states,
The mirrors displayed my subjects.

A junk drawer had no bottom.
I slept on a trampoline
And walked on crocodiles.

Troops attacked at all hours
And I gallantly defended.
If it was safe to cross,
I would let down my hair.

I was Cinderella.
I was Tinker Bell.

But, oh, how much more enchanting
To finally just be me.

*I compiled a collection of more than 150 works of poetry that I wrote during my teen years but unfortunately the only copy of that entire work was lost in the mail when I was just seventeen. I was devastated by the loss of those poems. Originally I thought only one poem remained but fortunately, over the years, I discovered duplicate copies of a few of those early poems so I am able to share this and the next ten poems that were written during my teen years. (JY)

THE THIEF

I would have survived if he had
Taken only my heart.
That has been stolen before.
But to take my poems,
To take my memories,
To take my careful verses.
"Was it the blushing blue..."
"When once I walked...."
My memory deceives me
And I cannot recreate the past.
Pages and pulses lost because
He was a cad, a thief, a
Wretched preying man.

He has vanished and hundreds of
Pages die with him.
I will never recreate those moments
Committed to paper for I am older
And no longer of the mind
That wrote them.
Only one poem remains of those
Immortalized sentiments.
Is that one self-conscious
Stanza an indication of what
He stole?

ANTI-WAR SONG

Five thousand men are dead.
Five thousand women won't wed,
Ten thousand parents grieve
Thirty thousand friends bereave.
One hundred thousand bodies will not mend.
When will it all end?

Five thousand men alone
Under an unmarked stone.
They do not see the trees
Surrounding their rotting knees.
Another Pyrrhic conquest
In the modern territorial contest.

ADOLESCENCE

There are many lavish prisons like this one:
Blue shutters with violets growing,
A detached garage and cobblestone path,
With lots of space and trees and sun.

Rocks I climbed as a carefree girl
Who later claimed them for explorers.
Who would see me splash paint or
My hidden laughter and pain?

Sharp-edged wire fences to avoid
But always tempting my friends and I.
And now the fence seems to
Get smaller as I get taller.

But that is then and not now
And the slamming door is locked.
No one knows who has swallowed
The key, if there is one.

My cell was once a carnival of cries:
Jump-jim-jo and "walk over the bridge,"
Imaginary soldiers and dancers.
Once it all seemed real to me.

But you would know what is gone if
You took the time to talk with me.
Whether we spoke of politics or drama
Or music, you know in one look.

Yet as I define it, it disappears
And it only returns when I remember

That it was even there.
It is translucent for once a
Twinkle's lost, so is the child.

WHO AM I?

There's a tear on my blouse,
Two on my cheeks.

Are they my tears?

But I thought I was a happy girl:
Pretty.
        Bright.
                Popular.

I'm just three sentimental drops of salt.

RESPONSIBILITY

They promised life would be sweet
But even flowers burst open and die.
I must see the leaves upon the trees
Even though naked branches quiver on bitter days.

Do I unwittingly scar frail beings
And fear that they will never heal?
Ah, but the blame is not mine.
It is Life, that fiendish freak,
So unpredictable and so harsh.

UNSPOKEN LOVE

Speak not the word,
Feel it in your heart,
Tell me with your eyes,
And I will answer with my gaiety.

Speak not the word,
Show me with your smile,
Declare it in your walk,
And I will answer
With my love.

THE CONE

Oh, cone of mine,
I found you on the grass.
How still you lay
Amidst all the whispering.
Now your perfect symmetry
Will travel in my hand,
Caressed by my fingers.

Oh, cone of mine,
I have broken one of your petals.
I cry for you.
Will you cry for me when
My heart is in pieces?

REVERSAL

If passion and friendship so often wane
Could the opposite also be true?
That lasting affection can regenerate
Again and again?

If spectacular starts often prove distressed
Why not believe in the reverse?
A colleague's nonchalance becomes respect,
An indifferent lover becomes obsessed.

Perhaps it is too simple to be true
But why not take that chance:
If disinterest can accumulate,
Maybe romantic love can ensue.

RARAVIS

I clutch his strength
And swallow life.

First a pebble,
Then a stone,
Anon a rock.

Raravis fills
An empty hole.

SECOND CHANCE

Give me back the years
I've blown away.
Let me do then
What I came to know
Today.

I AM A JEW

I am a Jew
Through and through
I am a Jew.

I am a Jew.
In my heart and in my soul
What are you?

Do you like me?
Even though I am a Jew.
Do you hate me?
Because I am a Jew?

I need to know.
Because the feelings run deep
I need to know.
Because of this latest slaughter I do weep.

I wept when I went to Dachau.
As a 25-year-old woman
And saw the remnants of the
Concentration camps.

I wept when I woke up Saturday.
To stories of mothers, children,
The elderly, men, and soldiers
Being slaughtered
In their homes
In their kibbutzim
At a peace concert.

For no other reason than that
They are Jews.
Like me
We are Jews.

We have been persecuted for three thousand years.
We have been hated and feared.
The jealousy runs deep.
The hate runs deep.
It is so unfounded.
Unless provoked.
We are a peace-loving people.
We are a kind and generous people.
We love our families.
We love our countries.

My grandfather witnessed
The pogrom in Ukraine which was
Then part of Russia.

The seniors were beheaded
in the synagogues
And he left and went to Brooklyn
And never went back to the Ukraine
Or to Russia
Or the synagogue again.
But his son, my father, embraced Judaism
And raised me to go to Hebrew school.

It is shocking and unimaginable to me to learn of
Beheadings but not in the early 1900s
In Russia
But last Friday in Israel
and of defenseless, innocent babies.

I have never been to Israel
But now more than ever I want to go
It is my land
The land of my forefathers
The land of my cousins and friends
The land of my fellow Jews.

Stop this madness
Stop this slaughter.
Stop this fighting.

I want peace in the Middle East
I want love and understanding.
I want to get along with everyone.
Arabs, Muslims, Christians, Buddhists,
Hindus, atheists, agnostics,
And other Jews.

I don't eat pork.
Not because I am Jew.
But because I am a vegetarian.

I don't go to synagogue on Sabbath
I'm not that religious..
But I went to schul on the
High Holy Days
Throughout my youth.

I had a Bat Mitzvah
My sons had a Bar Mitzvah
I love to dance the hora.
And to sing Hebrew songs
And to eat potato pancakes and

Other traditional Jewish dishes.

But most of all
Deep down and in my core
I am a Jew.
For that is what I was raised to be
Through all those years of Hebrew school
Learning the Hebrew language which I
Can still speak but can't still read.

So, what are you?
I am a Jew.
Can we be friends, too?

Written on Tuesday, October 10, 2023, on Day 3 of the Israel War on Hamas following the unprovoked attack and slaughter on October 7th of more than 1,000 of Jews inside of Israel at a music festival, in Kibbutzim, and in their homes.

Edited on Sunday, December 14, 2025, two years later, upon learning that 15 Jews were killed at a Hanukkah celebration the day before in an unprovoked attack on Bondi Beach in Sydney, Australia.

ABOUT THE AUTHORS

Fred Yager is the author of ten books including seven novels—three young adult novels —*Rex; Sound from a Star;* and *Cybersona* — and two mysteries, co-authored with his wife Jan—*Just Your Everyday People* and *Untimely Death*—Botanica, co-authored with their son Jeff, and the historical novel, The Asian Queen. Fred is also the co-author of two career reference books, co-authored with Jan—*Career Opportunities in the Publishing Industry* and *Career Opportunities in the Film Industry,* and *The Idiot's guide to Social Security*. His poetry about war is included in the anthology *The Healing Power of Creative Mourning: Poems*. For 13 years, Fred was a reporter and then an entertainment writer and movie critic for the Associated Press. He has worked as an editor for the Fox Seven O'clock News and he ran Merrill Lynch business television for seven years, among other corporate communications positions.

Fred majored in Psychology at CCNY (City College of New York) where he was a valedictorian candidate.

Jan Yager (the former J.L. – Janet Lee—Barkas) is the author or co-author of 70+ books with translations into 36 languages including the nonfiction titles *Friendshifts; When Friendship Hurts; Productive Relationships; The Fast Track Guide to Speaking in Public; Friendgevity; Work Less, Do More* (2nd edition); and *125 Ways to Meet the Love of Your Life; How to Finish Everything You Start; Time Masters: 11 Secrets to Greater Productivity and Life Fulfillment;* the novels *Justin Time for Love; The Pretty One; On the Run; Just Your Everyday People and Untimely Death (the last two co-authored with Fred),* and several children's books including *The Cantaloupe Cat* and *Fairy Tale Sequels, Book 2, The Three Little Pigs.*

Jan majored in art in college (Hofstra University), has a masters in criminal justice (Goddard College), did graduate work in art therapy (Hahnemann Medical College), and has a doctorate in sociology from The City University of New York Graduate Center (CUNY

Graduate Center). In addition to teaching at the college undergraduate and graduate level over the years including the University of Connecticut, Penn State, NYIT, John Jay College of Criminal Justice, William Paterson University, the New York Film Academy, and the University of South Florida (USF), among others.

She's also worked at major publishing companies, including Macmillan and Grove Press and has had her books published by such commercial and academic houses as Simon & Schuster, Scribner's, Prentice-Hall, Wiley, Aspen Publishing, Johns Hopkins University Press, and Doubleday. In 1996, she started her own publishing company, Hannacroix Creek Books, Inc. (https://www.hcbooks.us) celebrating its 30th year in 2026.

Jan coaches on topics of her expertise including time management, writing, getting published, foreign rights, and relationships including friendship. For Jan's availability for speaking or coaching opportunities, contact her at jyager@aol.com.

Fred and Jan Yager are married and the parents of two grown sons, Scott and Jeff. They have half a dozen grandchildren ranging in age from one to sixteen.

The Yagers are the co-authors or authors of completed original spec screenplays as well as screenplays based on their novels. If you are a producer, director, or actor with a production company and you want to consider optioning one or more of their screenplays, write to: hannacroix@aol.com

Fred and Jan Yager, November 2025
Photo credit: Jeff Yager

For more on the Yagers, go to:
https://www.fredandjanyager.net
https://www.drjanyager.com
https://www.hcbooks.us

If you are interested in having the Yagers read their poetry at your bookstore, library, poetry, author, literary festival, or book club, contact the Yagers with details about your event at jyager@aol.com

More poetry books from Hannacroix Creek Books, Inc.

The Healing Power of Creative Mourning: Poems deals with the themes of coping with illness, death, grief, loss, and bereavement. From the Preface by Fred Yager and Jan Yager: "...Creativity can help to fill the emotional void caused by a loss. It empowers you as you take that loss, whether it's because of terminal illness, death, or separation, and create something from it...But whether or not you write your own poetry, there is a cathartic benefit to reading the poems of others...."

The collection has poems by Fred Yager, Jan Yager, Priscilla Orr, Seth Alan Barkas, and Scott Yager. It also includes an Epilogue on coping with grief, selected references, and a list of resources.

What they're saying about this collection:
"In *The Healing Power of Creative Mourning* you'll quickly discover words written with logic that seems to touch the heart in ways that logic can't explain. I highly recommend this lovely book of poetry."
—Eva Shaw, Ph.D., author of *What To Do When A Loved One Dies*

In ***Losing the Horizon: Poems***, award-winning poet Priscilla Orr shares her feelings on love, aging, loss and death, as well as the comfort and courage we find in the natural cycle of the seasons—spring, summer, winter and fall. This is Orr's second collection of poetry. Her first collection is *Jugglers and Tides: Poems*.

Praise for *Losing the Horizon:*
"This is a moving, poignant collection from a mature voice at the top of her craft."
—Paul Genega, poet, *That Fall: New and Selected Poems*

"These poems, expressed with clarity, wisdom and grace, treat nostalgia without sentimentality. They come full circle, from the complexities of childhood to contemplation of aging and the ever-present specter of death, giving full measure to the persistent tug of grief on the human heart."
—Marina Antropow Cramer, Watchung Booksellers, Montclair, NJ

***Jugglers and Tides*** is Priscilla Orr's powerful and eloquent first collection. Here is the full range of Orr's penetrating, lyrical, and philosophical view of the world as she explores and probes loss, the mother-daughter relationship, childlessness, searching for love, fear, sexuality, loneliness, the father-daughter relationship, illness, and friendship.

Praise for *Jugglers and Tides*:
"…some of the best poetry being written today…Orr's work contains the inner music of good poetry and will prove a treat to all who discover her."
—Alan Caruba, *Bookviews*

"Orr's poetic voice is intensely personal, yet resonates with universal themes recognizable to the human experience of life and love and courage."
—*Wisconsin Bookwatch*

Novels by Fred and Jan Yager

Untimely Death, a psychological thriller, introduces a new sleuth, criminology professor Kimberly Stone. It explores the darkest depths of a human psyche showing how a nightmarish world of twisted sexuality evolves into murderous rage.

Praise for *Untimely Death*:

"The Yagers have written a winner."—Associated Press

"Fine book. A fascinating piece of work."
—Andrew M. Greeley, author, *Wages of Sin*

Just Your Everyday People, a suspense novel, deals with the potentially dire costs of silence.

"The friendship between two married couples begins to unravel when one of the wives seduces a stranger in a bar. Blackmail, betrayal and murder ensue, and the danger seems to come from all directions."—*Publishers Weekly*

"*A* sneaky little thriller that explores the underside of suburban life in a way that contrasts the mundane with the horrible…"—John Lutz, best-selling novelist, *Single White Female*

Selected Novels by Fred Yager

Sound from a Star
Fifteen-year-old Devon Turner, a junior in high school, thinks he's picked up music from outer space on his satellite dish. He records the sound, takes it to an astronomer who shares it with a musicologist. Within 24 hours, the sound is being played on radio stations everywhere. The music has a powerful vibration that can be used to heal or to destroy. But where is the music coming from?

Praise for *Sound from a Star*:
"a deftly written, original, and thoroughly entertaining read offering an engaging story that will grip the total attention of teen readers from first page to last."
— *Midwest Book Review*

Rex
This novel is an adventure about an unusual friendship in which a young boy, whose paleontologist parents are missing, finds himself in possession of something long believed to be extinct.

What they're saying about *Rex:*
"In *Rex,* by Fred Yager (co-author of *Untimely Death*), 11-

187

year-old Davy Ross's paleontologist parents go missing from a dig on Mount Kilimanjaro, and he finds a mysterious egg among their belongings. When a tiny dinosaur hatches, Davy has to protect him from an unscrupulous professor, return the tyrannosaurus to its jungle home and locate his missing parents."
— *Publishers Weekly*

"The author, a screenwriter, has presented a very visual story that's fast-paced and full of action...."
—*School Library Journal*

Cybersona
In an extreme case of identity theft, a computer genius who has recently become a quadriplegic when caught in the crossfire of a gang shootout uses an Internet game called "Cybersona" to take over the body of another player, a recently-fired science teacher, to get revenge on those responsible for his paralysis. In an effort to get his body back, the teacher takes over the body of the next player who signs on; that player turns out to be a ten-year-old boy.

From *Heartland Reviews*:
"The pace of this novel is frenetic. As fast as the story develops, it still allows the reader to reflect on the aspects of revenge and justice tempered by forgiveness and compassion. We rated this excellent story four hearts."

Jan Yager's selected novels

Just in Time for Love
A Novella
2026
(Available in e-book and print versions)
214 pages

Based on the screenplay, "No Time for Love," co-written by Fred Yager and Jan Yager, this novella tells the tale of what happens when Kate Hellman, a time management consultant and college professor who is often late, is on a frantic search for Mr. Right before her biological clock runs out.

Praise for *Just in Time for Love:*
"A real page turner—great fun—a whirlwind romance—whirlwind read as well!
—Sue M., book club organizer

The Pretty One

Psychologist Dr. Emily Taylor seemed to have it all: she's thin, attractive, happily married with children, with a successful therapy practice and writing career. Then she's interviewed on a major morning talk show to discuss her bestseller as being in the limelight catapults Emily on a food binge. As her weight climbs over 200, she realizes she has to deal with the underlying causes—the secret she has been keeping about what happened to her beginning at the age of 10 —that may be behind the compulsive overeating and bingeing that she is battling. This uplifting novel will forever impact how you view your own or someone else's weight-related challenges.

Praise for *The Pretty One*
"Bravely takes you to the heart and hell of a compulsive overeater yet offers hope for healing too."
—Dr. Cynthia Allison, psychologist

"Captures the emotional ups and downs that accompany the main character's battles with her weight...."
—Leigh Cohn, Editor-in-Chief, *Eating Disorders: The Journal of Treatment and Prevention*

"*The Pretty One* released powerful emotions in me. I couldn't put it down." (a reader)

Journals

Birthday Tracker and Journal is a special place to record important birthdays for family, friends, and others, month by month. It includes an informative introduction on birthday celebration traditions and lists birthday birthstones and flowers by month for gift-giving considerations. There is also a place to keep track of birthday cards or presents that you send, or receive, lined blank pages for your birthday reflections, and a place for birthday photos. Four-color illustrations by author/artist Jan Yager appear throughout. This unique book is a perfect gift or for one's own use to organize this special birthday information.

Available in hardcover and paperback editions.

Personal Journal
This journal of blank ruled pages provides a handy place for writing down your thoughts, notes, or observations. The cover of this journal is from an original collage by author/artist Jan Yager.

Available in hardcover and paperback editions.

Selected Nonfiction Titles by Jan Yager

In Love and Work captures love as it is actually lived— alongside careers, creativity, ambition, and everyday life demands. *How to Have a Happy Romantic Relationship* continues that conversation, providing practical insights and tips for couples who want love that lasts *and* works.

Written by sociologist Jan Yager, Ph.D., and drawing on decades of research, coaching, and teaching related college courses, this book explores what helps romantic relationships thrive over time: communication that connects, independence that strengthens rather than threatens love, and shared experiences that build resilience when life gets complicated. You'll find playlists of songs to listen or dance to, month-by-month activity suggestions, prompts to speak or write your answers to, an extensive resource section, poems, two short stories, and lots more. Color photographs and artwork reproductions throughout.

Productive Relationships: 57 Strategies for Building Stronger Business Connections is a practical guide to developing productive business relationships to help you get along at work whether you work for a major corporation, a small business, or are a self-employed entrepreneur or freelancer.

A follow-up to Yager's well-received international hit, *Who's That Sitting at My Desk?*—but this book stands alone—Yager covers everything from dealing with workplace bullies— coworkers as well as bosses—as well as negative and positive types you may encounter at work and how to cope with each one, workplace violence, and using social media more effectively. The author's bosses have included legendary publisher Barney Rosset, Pulitzer Prize-winning author Norman Mailer, academic chairs, and many executives.
Published by Hannacroix Creek Books, Inc., 2011

Praise for *Productive Relationships*:
"Jan Yager's *Productive Relationships* is a valuable resource for getting into the modern day workplace and for happily remaining there as well."
—Christopher "Kip" Forbes, Vice Chairman, Forbes

Available in hardcover, trade paperback, and e-book editions.

HANNACROIX CREEK BOOKS, INC.

titles are available at local or online retailers as well as directly from the publishing company

Original drawing with marker and pastel by Jan Yager

For more information, go to:

http://www.hcbooks.us